soul scan

FACING HARD REALITIES TO HEAL WHAT'S BROKEN

VANESA ALCANTARA

SPEAK FIRE
PUBLISHING

Contents

Dedication

To the women who at some point have allowed me into their lives. Thank you for gifting me the privilege of knowing you and seeing you for who you are. Thank you for allowing me to do life with you, hold your hand through difficult times and help you with scanning your own soul. You know who you are.

To my husband for sharing in the blood, sweat and many tears we've put into this. Thank you for encouraging my soul when I needed it the most. And to my children, you are a huge part of why I seek to constantly do the soul work, break generational patterns and seek to be more like Jesus.

Lastly, to my hero. My everything, Jesus. Thank you for being present, faithful, loving, and constant in my life. You've shown me that with You, healing and growth are possible. I owe you everything, May this book set women free and launch them into a life of wholeness, renewed purpose, and fullness in Christ.

Foreword

This book is proof of a battle that has been raging with you Vanesa (the author called to write this book), me (the editor, called to polish it), and their families for at least the entirety of 2023 and 2024.

This is how I personally know that this book is going to set women free because as an editor, who is a public speaker, you know the moment when someone touches your heart and doesn't let you go—God has highlighted you in my vision.

Vanesa, you have easily been one of those dynamos in my list of women. You are someone who lights a fire of His presence within me, even when we're talking about mundane things. I see how hard you seek after the Father's stamp of excellence and approval *on this project*. You do what The Lord tells you, and when you have seen that you were wrong, you were **quick to repent** and change course, whether or not it is convenient, comfortable, or private—even if that repentance takes years (in some cases that redirect was/is HARRRRD)!

I thank the Lord for you, and I thank you for making this testimony into a chain breaker for other women!

I ask You, Lord, to bless Vanesa and her family now as she moves forward with this book, because I know of the battle that she faced in the minutes (and I know of the battle that I face EVERY TIME I start trying to help her), which just tells me that the devil doesn't want this book to get out and set other women free. And so I set this prayer over anyone involved in this scribal birthing—that they be protected from any plans of the enemy concerning this book and their involvement with it!

In Jesus' name, Amen!!!

Tiffany Vakilian

Founder and CEO

Speak Fire Publishing

Introduction

Women across the globe are desperate for a change in their world. Work-Life. Home-Life. Relationship-Life. Wife-Life. Mom-Life. Sister-Life. ALL the roles we play—we don't always feel like we are functioning at our highest potential. The everyday grind has taken a toll on us, leaving us stripped of hope and peace as we continually sacrifice ourselves for others.

Even in the church, some women run ragged, empty, joyless, and lonely, but they keep pushing through their days to keep up with appearances. Unfortunately, some women have even convinced themselves that this is *just the way things will always be*, or *this is just the way I am.*

Friend, this is not living life to its fullest.

You may feel overwhelmed by the constant demands of life. The weight of everything you need to do is feeling heavier and heavier, leaving you ineffective, powerless, and throbbing with pain deep in your soul. I'm talking about down in the places of your soul that you weren't even aware existed! You probably picked up this book with the halfway attempt to make sense of your life.

Maybe you're looking for hope because your situation seems hopeless. You feel like you've lost yourself within all your priorities and feel stuck in a cycle of disappointment and frustration. The weight presses you deeper underwater, and even when you come up for air, you feel like you can't escape the busyness and the need to please everyone around you.

Girl, it's exhausting!

You put others first while suppressing your emotional needs. And maybe reading this book is your attempt to finally respond to your soul's desperate cry. You need someone to sit with you, look you in the eyes, and tell you, "Your pain matters to God. You can stop running now."

In this book, I want to help you scan your soul. Yes, scan your soul.

I want you to take the next 30 days to focus on some deep work within your heart and mind to help you deal with the hard things, heal from those things, and then grow beyond them! I want to help you face the hard realities of your life, uncover how pain and fear keep you from self-awareness, which can lead you to temporary fixes. I want to help you introduce the closed-off parts of your soul to Jesus—the Gentle Healer and the Great Redeemer of your story. I want to help you connect the real you to the real Jesus and ignite an authentic relationship between you and Him. Let's take the time to identify the wounds, lies, and habits that keep you stuck. For the next month or so, I will help you sort through the unhealthy narratives you believe about yourself and allow God's Truth to set you free!

To face your hard realities and uncover your great need for a Savior, you must look deeper into your soul. That's why this book is here. God told me to write it FOR YOU! The Lord has given me a charge, an assignment: I am to train women to deal, heal and grow by scanning their souls.

But this concept is not foreign to God. Psalm 139 talks about it quite clearly.

Search me [thoroughly], O God, and know my heart; Test me and know my anxious thoughts; and see if there is any wicked or hurtful way in me, and lead me in the everlasting way. Psalm 139: 23-24 AMP

You may have picked up this book because you, too, have felt the nagging ache in your heart. Your deep pain and wounding has shown up in various ways throughout your life, and you're unsure what to do.

Welp, you've picked up the right book!

This book will serve as a divine interruption to your daily struggles and will give you tools to grow closer to God while facing your everyday battles as the full you the Creator made. It will help you live as the empowered woman of faith God has called you to be, even while facing the great demise of self—a demise vital to you if you are to live the life God wants you to live.

I want to challenge you for the next 30 days. And even if it takes a bit longer, it's okay, Sis! Take your time, but *please do the work!* It's the only way to get to the other side of your healing and greatness. The volume of work you put in will be the volume of transformation you will experience. I encourage you to set time aside daily for this metamorphosis.

Sit somewhere you can focus with your journal and your Bible ready to join you. Read along and answer questions (or respond to powerful, freeing comments) you probably have not thought about. Remove yourself from all distractions. I encourage you to take on a fast (which means abstaining from things you enjoy, like food, sugar, social media, electronics, meats, etc.) because this is worth the sacrifice! Whatever that thing is for you, let it be a stake in the ground for a time as you take this soul work seriously.

You can do this!

My prayer is that this book will be a bridge for you. I want to see you go from living in fear to thriving in freedom.

I want you to face your hard realities to allow God to heal what is broken. It's time to lean into safety and security in Jesus as you discover who and Whose you are. You can do this! Let's cross this bridge together and ask God for a soul scan.

Are you ready?!

Let's go!

Interruption

ARE YOU DOWN FOR THE JOURNEY TO DEAL, HEAL, AND GROW?

"FACING THE HARDEST THING CAN SOMETIMES BE THE BEST THING."
— VANESA ALCANTARA

It was late at night and we were arguing (or what I like to call having "intense fellowship") about something I can't remember.

But this was the moment that changed my life.

Prior to this, narratives about myself that I adopted over the years had become permanent tapes replaying in my head. Over the years, I learned to be fiercely independent, not only because it was a picture of strength, but because I was terrified at the thought of putting my trust in someone else. These mindsets and thought patterns caused me to think I needed to stand up for myself, even if it meant dragging my husband down with my words. Because if tearing him down wouldn't build him up, then what would?

As I sat on the futon in our small two-bedroom apartment, the walls closed in on me as he stood across from me near the entrance door. My heart was pounding, and the knot in my throat grew tighter as I desperately tried to keep myself from crying (again).

I asked him, "What am I doing wrong?! Please. Just tell me what you want me to do, or at least tell me, *what you're thinking*!"

He paused. He just stood there in his basketball shorts, tank top, and a stank face on top of that! The humming sound of the fridge was the soundtrack of that moment. We were both physically and emotionally exhausted from arguing late into the night about a looming topic that had gone unspoken for the last four and a half years. He looked at me from a distance. Afraid, yet gearing up for my usual over-the-top reaction. And with a defeated tone, he sternly yet calmly uttered words that pierced my heart.

"Babe," he said, "I think you're a disrespectful wife..."

The humming sound from the fridge grew louder as I sat there in shock. At first, my insides wanted to stand up and prove him wrong! Make him see I am respectful!

"*DEFEND YOURSELF!*" I hollered in my head. But honestly, I sat there and said nothing. Profound silence joined us as we looked at one another, sinking into the moment. I dropped deeper into that futon, wishing it would swallow me whole. I DID NOT see this coming!

But it was the start of something beautiful.

Have you ever been completely thrown off by something your spouse did or said? Perhaps it was your best friend, parent, sibling, or another person who said something that pierced your heart and froze you in time. That searing spotlight on an internal issue (which you most likely already knew about) made you pause, despite yourself. Not only did it take your breath away; but the person who called out the issue forced you to face it without the *avoidance* or *delay* tactics you may have in place.

My husband's words completely blindsided me, but I knew he was right.

That moment with my husband helped me confront more than just the issues in our marriage; it revealed other matters I kept ignoring. My husband's words made me face the enormous gap in my relationship with him, and in my relationship with God.

As a woman of faith, I know that the state of my relationship with God sets the tone for everything else in my life. That moment exposed just how much I had put my relationship with Christ on the back burner.

The room was silent, but my racing thoughts were loud. Those thoughts said:

This isn't how it's supposed to go.
I thought he was the problem.
Oh, My Goodness. What if it IS me?
How did I miss this?
You are an idiot.
Wow... I feel SO far from God.

Often, the most painful moments of our lives reveal the places in us that still need healing. My husband called my brokenness out right there, witnessed by a humming refrigerator.

The distance I allowed between God and myself left me vulnerable. And I was moving along, going unchecked, unsearched, and unaware. The more I realized how far I'd strayed from a humble and genuinely intimate relationship with God, the more shame and desperation settled in my being.

The pain we feel is only a symptom of a more complex inner reality. The aftermath of painful experiences can make us feel vulnerable and exposed to the people closest to us. There is an impulse to run away from those issues (and hurts) which are taking root to protect ourselves from the hurt. Our need for control intensifies because we feel out of control. And slowly, we begin to turn to things that will not serve us. We end up coping in toxic ways. These false emotional protectors only numb us and keep us from connecting with God—our Provider, Source, Creator, and Healer. Numbness is proof we've gone too far down this road and it's a significant factor that keeps us from seeing the Truth. In the end, we bring more pain to our already hurting souls.

The discomfort we experience indicates that we have internal injuries and wounds that need healing.

The Truth is, I got lost in my fears and unmet expectations. I lost sight of the One person who knows me intimately and knows how to calm my anxious heart. I lost sight of Jesus. He showed me how great the gap between Him and I had grown. And the more expansive the gap became, the less capable I was of receiving His healing and the ability to love others without overly protecting myself.

Sometimes, we don't even realize our need to deal with our emotional baggage until these symptoms begin wreaking havoc in our lives and relationships. Crisis and breakdown are often the onramps to our most meaningful spiritual and emotional work. Marriage struggles, health challenges, bankruptcy, or other crises have brought it on. But God uses these challenges to show us the places where He wants to show up and bring you into deeper wholeness, well-being, and purpose. Unfortunately, we often take matters into our own hands, hoping it brings us closer to hope and safety. Yet, more often than not, we dig ourselves deeper into a pit and find ourselves even further away from the Source where we find our healing. It is He who informs our souls of who we are. Unfortunately, many of us have only met the survival mode version of ourselves. Our Christ-centered identities get lost in the challenges of life. The gap seems vast, the pit feels bottomless, and hope seems lost.

But there is a Rescuer for our souls ready to save us.

One of two things happens when we find ourselves in a spiritual and emotional breakdown; we move toward healing or self-preservation. In those moments, the best option is to allow yourself to move toward the healing opportunity God is setting before you and watch how the transformation will begin. You cannot accomplish this transformative work alone. On the other hand, when you choose self-preservation, you miss out on healing, change, and getting closer to the One who truly sees you, knows you, and can love you right out of your brokenness.

That night in our living room, I didn't know it, but I chose healing as the sadness overcame me. Not only was I hurting my husband with my words and actions, but I also began to realize that I was aching on the inside and didn't know it. The truth is, I had allowed an old fear of hardship to consume my heart. I lived by the fear that I would be left vulnerable and without security if I didn't stay in constant control.

I feel blessed to have been raised by immigrant parents who defied all odds to make a life for themselves in the United States. The flip side to that blessing is that I grew up hearing about their many heartbreaks and struggles from the time I was a little girl. Constantly hearing about these challenges and stressors filled me with fear and sadness. As a child, I remember looking forward to the day when I could work and feel the peace and security not afforded to my parents. But these inner vows left no room in my marriage to grow and build together with my husband.

Instead, my throbbing wound caused me to become someone who tore into her husband instead of building him up. And this happened publicly and privately. I constantly talked down to him and highlighted *all* the ways he failed to hit the mark as a husband. Worse, I tried to mother him when he needed a partner, a friend, or a lover.

Unfortunately, his efforts to try and be the best husband and leader he could be were never enough to silence my established stronghold of fears that were firmly in place way before we even met! Rather than allowing the perfect love of God to drive out all my worries, I bought into the prevalent lies of our world today that say:

Men are children and are unable to wear the pants.
Your desires to be led, covered, and loved simply don't matter.
We must settle for shallow love where our hearts find no shelter.
It's time to put on your big-girl panties.
You will have to lead yourself due to his inability to lead you.
Be careful not to have big feelings—you are too much.
Men already see us as too much to handle.
You must be the boss.
If you don't stand up and lead your marriage, all you've worked so hard for will be lost.

These are just some of the lies I bought into. Have you said some of these to yourself?

My heart breaks for the self-talk so many women have endured for so long. Whether you are married, single, divorced, widowed, or in any other relationship, these are terrible lies deeply rooted in their hearts.

I'm grateful that God, in His gentleness and patience, got a hold of my heart.

I had to humble myself and ask God and my husband for forgiveness. In many ways, that was the easy part. The real work came when I had to lay my fears at the foot of the cross, repent of my need for control, and acknowledge that there was more brokenness and dysfunction inside me than I had fully understood. Taking care of all that was the hardest, most beautiful work. And now I regularly check in on my mind, will, and emotions.

I call it a *Soul Scan*.

I had to scan my soul and identify the bruises and broken areas so that I could deal with, heal from, and grow beyond the pain. I soon learned that soul scanning would become a regular part of my life and is truly a work of the Spirit.

Every time we perform a soul scan, God meets us in our place of brokenness with His love, peace, and power. He is ever ready to make us well and whole, but it starts with our willingness to inspect and acknowledge the wounded parts of our souls.

God hears you. He sees you, and He knows you're tired.

Friend, if I were in front of you right now, I would come a bit closer, grab your hand, look you in the eye and say to you, "I see you, and we're in this together." I know your pain and anger feel louder than anything else, but there is so much more available to you as a child of God! There is hope for your future, your soul's transformation, your mind's renewal, and healing for what's broken. But more than anything else, friend, you are not alone." Then I would wipe my own tears, straighten my shoulders and give you the hard Truth.

I'd say something like this:

"REAL strength is found in our Source—Jesus, and Him alone. Your strength is not real strength until it comes from Him." Then I'd ask you with sincerity and a slight break in my voice, "Would you allow me to journey with you? You will pay a price for going on this journey. There will be a sacrifice of time, commitment, and dedication while going after some soul-level healing. But it will be so worth it in the end. Let's walk this out together."

7

Chapter 1 Challenge: Get Started

Write out a prayer inviting God to help you *deal, heal,* and *grow.*
Don't worry about what it sounds like. Write an Honest prayer
without judging your words.

_____

_____

_____

_____

_____

_____

_____

_____

_____

_____

_____

_____

_____

_____

_____

_____

_____

_____

_____

_____

_____

Phase I

DEAL WITH IT...
CHAPTERS 2-4

Welcome to phase one of your inner healing journey! This is the phase where we dump out your emotional bag (purse, bookbag, whatever bag you want to imagine) in order to sort through the areas you've been carrying for years that have been causing you pain and have become a burden you can no longer bear. When you are aware of what is in there- you are able to see what needs healing in order for you to grow beyond what's been holding you back all this time. This is soul scanning: helping you *deal, heal & grow.*

Are you ready? Let's go!

Soul Buckets

WHAT'S IN THERE?

"WHAT WELLS DO YOU TURN TO WHEN YOUR SOUL IS THIRSTY?"
— VANESA ALCANTARA

I love the old hymn called *It Is Well with My Soul*. But sometimes, I wonder if we should switch the order of words to ask ourselves, "Is it well with my soul?" Sometimes I've thought about it mid-song, "Is it well... with your soul, Vanesa?" Friend, it is only well with your soul when Jesus is the WELL you turn to. When you don't turn to Jesus, the well of living water, the Source of Life, it can't be well with your soul.

As a kid, when going to someone's house my mom would give us the rundown while we were in the car. She would turn around and say, "Don't you dare ask for a drink or food! I fed you at home, so you're not hungry!" Once we would sit in the living room, the women would begin to chit-chat, then the lady of the house would come over and ask, "Do you want something to drink? Can I get you anything?"

Even if we wanted some water, we were terrified to say a word! There is a deep thirst-like desire within each of us because we all have soul buckets that only God can fill. *You are not too needy.* You are not too far from God. You are a beloved daughter of God whose soul buckets He wants to fill! And He is not in the business of withholding a drop of that living water, so the "Yes" is clear and unending.

In the Bible, King David wrote many of the Psalms, and I particularly love how he describes his thirst for God.

Psalms 42:1-3 NIV says,

> *As the deer pants for streams of water, so my soul pants for you, my God. My soul thirsts for God, for the living God. When can I go and meet with God? My tears have been my food day and night, while people say to me all day long, "Where is your God?*

Psalm 63:1 NIV says,

> *You, God, are my God, earnestly I seek you; I thirst for you, my whole being longs for you, in a dry and parched land where there is no water.*

Your thirst indicates the places in you that God needs to fill. He delights in meeting you and quenching your thirst, sister. He wants to fill your soul bucket!

Now put yourself in this story for a moment. Let's pretend that you are a guest at my house. You're sitting in our living room, having a great time. Maybe my husband Ernesto comes in with a charcuterie board. *Sidenote: that man loves a charcuterie board!* As we are all chit-chatting and laughing, I lean over to you and say,

"Hey, can I get you something? Are you thirsty?" Suddenly, you feel this tense sensation of some random person looking straight at you from across the room and sternly answering for you, "No, thank you."

Can you feel the sinking feeling in your stomach as you imagine that? Can you feel the conflicting shame and disappointment that accompanies your thirst? Is it possible that you carry that sinking feeling with you all the time?

That is the lying voice of shame. I know I hear it at times and that voice constantly needs to be shut down!

Someone who also discovered the true nature of her thirst was the Samaritan woman Jesus spoke to in John chapter 4. The thirsty soul we now famously know as the woman at the well has an encounter with Jesus that changed her life forever. In the story, we find a woman fetching water at the hottest time of the day, where she can avoid other women's judgmental glances. While gathering physical water, she encounters Jesus, who helps her see that she has a deep thirst that man has been unable to satisfy (though she has tried). We learn that she has had five husbands and that the man she was with at that time wasn't even her husband. The woman at the well was thirsty for something other than water when Jesus met her there. She was, in fact, thirsty for a more profound provision. Her soul bucket (or vessel) was empty and Jesus was the only one who could provide what she needed. Jesus is the living water that satisfies our inner thirst. What if her internal voice of shame kept her from leaning in the conversation? What if the ladies of the town were there, and told her, "No! You can't have any water!" Would this have caused her to walk away unfulfilled?

Maybe you too feel ashamed for being thirsty while the eyes of culture, family, or friends, or even the stern look of your internal self, tells you that you shouldn't be needy. Maybe shame is the one answering "no" for you because you carry an unspoken rule that you should not be an inconvenience. Perhaps, even though you are so clearly dehydrated, you continuously try to convince yourself not to partake in what God offers you because the "look" of culture says that "strong people don't *need* that kind of water."

Instead of listening to those opposing voices, I want you to imagine that, at that exact moment, Jesus starts speaking to you.

"I know you're thirsty," he says lovingly. "I know you're searching. I know you've already drunk from other water wells at your home, and they don't taste right or fill you up. But I am the living water you are truly thirsty for. Let me fill your soul bucket."

Maybe you have felt that deep draw sometimes, late at night, when you lay your head on your pillow, unable to sleep. Maybe your thoughts run wild, and you feel a gaping hole inside your soul.

That, my sister, is thirst.

Your soul bucket is empty, my friend.

You've been pretending to be ok. But your life has become a desert, and you're living in a season of significant drought! We can sing songs and smile, moving along mindlessly. Sometimes we forget to ask ourselves if we even mean the words we say or the smile we've put on.

It's a sobering question when you ask yourself, "Do I truly believe this?"

Knowing Jesus, He would have made it into an even more beautiful lesson of love and soul care. The well was a beautiful representation of who Jesus wanted to be in her life. He wanted to be her well of life.

My Sister, the same goes for you.

What if you were thirsty, and you were trying to fill your soul bucket. Ask yourself, what wells do you turn to when your soul is thirsty? What do you try to put in your bucket? Is it Jesus, the Living Water? Or do you turn to toxic wells which, instead of filling you up, keep your soul thirsty and sick? When we are in pain, we might incorrectly seek something temporary. Our unhealthy habits will constantly lead us to drink from contaminated wells instead of the Well of Living Water.

Remember, thirst is a God-given thing but not all things are meant to fill your soul bucket! God created us for connection with Him. We will never truly satisfy our thirst without Living Water. The woman at the well had tried to fulfill her own needs in her own way by having five different husbands. There were needs that were known and many that were unknown to her that led her to hop from one relationship to another. It was clear that her thirst ran deep. It's beautiful to see how in the midst of her brokenness, she encountered Christ, the well that never runs dry.

So how can we identify our thirst? In what ways have we been trying to fill our soul buckets instead of allowing God to quench our thirst? Without any judgment, let's think about our desires for a moment. We have unique desires, hopes, and dreams in our hearts. Take some time to really think about what has captivated your heart over the years.

Perhaps you were captivated by the idea of falling in love. Or you thought having children and caring for your home would "fill your bucket." Maybe you thought that following your passion and carving out a path would lead you toward a successful career that would bring you happiness.

But what happens when you've put your hope, trust, dependence, resources, blood, sweat, and tears into all those desires, and your bucket is *still empty?*

Maybe at first, you found happiness. The newness that comes with learning about yourself and discovering who you are can be thrilling. Maybe you've created beautiful memories throughout the years and found that you loved your journey, only to discover that you still felt empty, despite all the good things. The gaping hole was still aching in ways you could not understand. Maybe you started having new doubts and challenges, painful arguments, or mishaps in communication. Your bucket might have spilled some of those precious joys, leaving you disappointed and emptier than you thought you'd be.

Fast forward a few more years, and you now hold onto an empty bucket with anger and resentment. Your life no longer fills you like it once did. You now stand brokenhearted with your empty bucket, trying to figure out who's to blame for the pain you feel from loss and betrayal within a particular relationship.

Sometimes we can even trace these pain-points back to our childhood.

Unfulfilled expectations of feeling safe, protected, emotionally covered, loved, and cared for have been disappointing.

You see, those wounds may point to the faults of others, but they also point to the rich provisions available to us in God. He is the only bucket filler, so turn to Him!

Maybe our need for comfort helps us form the prayers that pull on God, who is The Comforter. The voids we experience have been strategically allowed by our Creator. So, maybe our need for healing helps us discover Jesus, The Healer. Without our pain and disappointment, we could miss out on truly knowing God's love for us more fully. Look into your longings and you will see Your Heavenly Father smiling right there.

He's been waiting the whole time.

Our longings teach us what to ask God for in order to *deal* with our brokenness. Though God may allow some of the pain and brokenness we experience, *He never leaves us there*. Jesus always makes a way to remove all the debris left from past pain and old wounds so that our Heavenly Father can heal and fill us until our cup overflows.

I love how King David puts it in Psalm Chapter 23 NIV:

> *The Lord is my shepherd, I lack nothing.*
> *He makes me lie down in green pastures, he leads me*
> *beside quiet waters,*
> *he refreshes my soul. He guides me along the right paths*
> *for his name's sake.*

*Even though I walk through the darkest valley, I will
fear no evil, for you are with me; your rod and your staff,
they comfort me.
You prepare a table before me in the presence of my enemies. You anoint my head with oil; my cup overflows.
Surely your goodness and love will follow me all the
days of my life, and I will dwell in the house of the Lord
forever.*

My Sister, nothing and no one can fill our soul buckets like Jesus.

No amount of money or success can make us whole. We cannot make any external source responsible for filling the deepest parts of who we are. God created you to be a recipient of His perfect, divine, and eternal love. And nothing in this world can quench that thirst. Only Jesus.

Now, even when we confront our thirst and acknowledge that only God can fill our soul buckets, at one point or another, we all face the bitter reality that God's ways are not always to our liking. What happens when God's good and perfect will seems "off"? What happens when God allows more pain than what we would choose? What happens when God doesn't seem to respond the way we would like or as quickly as we believe He should?

In these moments of disillusionment, we often see where our sinful humanity can get in the way. Rather than waiting on the Lord and trusting his timing and provision, we often create our own resources and make our own way in the desert. We drag around our empty buckets and attempt to fill them with sand, pursuing life's pleasures and accomplishments. We poison our soul buckets by positioning ourselves to receive as much as we can from the tangible resources and people around us. In this pursuit of provision, we often find the gateway to idolatry.

These other sources inevitably become idols in our life, making it harder to deal with the thirst we felt in the first place.

But what do soul buckets have to do with idols?

I am glad you asked.

When we think of idols, we often associate them with gold statues and carved items that people bow down to and worship. However, not every idol takes on this form. More often than not, the idols we enthrone in our hearts don't always start as idols. Sometimes the idols in our lives are the temporary fixes we cling to in times of great fear or desperation. It can be food, work, our children, shopping, entertainment, or even religion. What starts as an innocent attempt to fill our soul bucket with hope and happiness can quickly become a turning of our backs to God in pursuit of other sources that we think will more quickly fill our deepest gaping holes. But our soul buckets were not made to be filled by temporal things. It's a simple, but powerful fact. He is jealous for our love. God desires to provide for those places in our hearts, mind, and spirit with Himself.

By means of idolatry, no matter how innocently it started, we clog the God-shaped holes in our souls with artificial junk. We are often guilty of idolatry whenever we direct our attention, affection, and obsession to anything but Jesus. And none of us are exempt. Some-times we idolize relationships, jobs, and vain goals. Sometimes, even our sinful habits become idols. We get so consumed with getting our needs met in tangible ways that we become unwilling to walk in faith and trust God, who supplies all our needs according to His riches in glory[1].

To receive the fullness God created you to receive, you must allow God to help you clear out the cheap knockoffs that take up room in place of your Heavenly Father. We are all created with a desire to feel secure, pursued, and loved. If God indeed is the

1. Philippians 4:19

manufacturer of our souls, the author and the finisher of our faith[2], and the Creator of our innermost being, then He would surely know us at depths and ends that we don't even know ourselves.

If that is the case, we cannot look for fulfilment in anything else but Him, no matter how good and generous it seems.

Of course, God uses several avenues to provide and meet our needs. He often works through several key relationships to supply provisions for us. Still, we must recognize that God is the one who orchestrates these provisions, and the fulfillment we receive should lead us back to Him.

Without even realizing we are incorrectly filling our soul buckets, we begin to place specific responsibilities on other people. We then haphazardly *require them* to fill us and task them with sustaining our joy and peace. Then, when they fail, we point the finger at God (with bitterness, like He did it to us). And rather than repenting with humility and returning to Jesus, we try again to fill our buckets with other people and alternatives. This is how easy it is for us to become depressed and bitter, because we are so unfulfilled.

And yet, in the same breath, we ask God to *bless our new idols.*

The more our expectations go unmet, the bigger the disappointment. The bigger the disappointment, the more tempted we are to turn to idols.

We don't always recognize it, but our hidden expectations are often at the root of our sadness and emptiness. They ultimately become the droplets at the bottom of the bucket that we spew out toward God in resentment.

Maybe this is what the people of Israel experienced when God delivered them from Egyptian slavery and led them into a desert when their leader Moses went up to Mt. Sinai (Exodus 19-32 NIV). When the people saw Moses taking so long to return, they feared that something had happened to him, and God was no longer with them. So, they made for themselves a golden calf because they

---

2. Hebrews 12:2

wanted a god to go before them. And in a short time, they turned their worship and affection toward this false god instead of the God who delivered them from bondage and could provide all their needs.

How often do we do the same?

In our desperate and fearful "waiting for God," we become impatient and make personal provisions. We act out, instead of trusting that God's provision and timing are perfect. It's time that we identify our false gods and cast down our idols. This is what "dealing with it" looks like. Just like so many of us; the woman at the well needed to deal with more than just her sin. She needed to allow Jesus to point out the gaping hole underneath her sin. She was continuously drawn to satiating a need for closeness with the men in her life. When all along, God was the only one who would fill her God-shaped hole.

Friend, you need to know something, and I need you to brace yourself for this truth.

God does not center His will and priorities for your life around your happiness.

If God joined you in your goal of focusing on your happiness, it would cheapen the greater treasures He has in store for you. Why would He contaminate your bucket like that?

His will for your life is not mere happiness. It is holiness. Let me repeat that. God's will for your life is HOLINESS. And holiness is forged through the suffering of death to self. You can only access His greater treasures by knowing Christ and trusting Him outside your preferences and comfort zones. I assure you that the result will lead you to something better than happiness.

I'm talking about filling your soul bucket with JOY.

True, unspeakable joy and a peace that surpasses all understanding are yours for the taking. Comfort like you've never known and confidence rooted in Him are waiting to be poured into your bucket! Unconditional love is, of course, on tap.

But we only get there by allowing Him to lead the way, even when it offends our flesh and denies our convenience. Seeing our sufferings as opportunities to know and trust God more deeply is a vital hope to hang onto because the truth is that some of our circumstances might never change. Some people might never grow or become capable of loving and supporting us well. God might not heal some of our illnesses on this side of heaven.

Try to see that through His eyes for just a moment.

What if the change God is most interested in begins with you? What if the great work God intends with your circumstance is to help you become less selfish? Imagine how your soul bucket (consider it your vessel) would look on the other side of that? What if the great miracle God has prepared in your turmoil is your new capacity to love as Christ does? New soul bucket capacity is possible! But as long as the goal is your happiness, you will miss all the riches and fellowship with Christ that you can only access through the pain and growth that happens when you release your comfort and pursue your holiness.

Maybe the very suffering you're asking God to take away is creating the open door to know God more intimately. Your pain may be helping you experience Jesus more deeply as He reveals the most remarkable and holy angles of who He is in light of your circumstances. As difficult as it is to trust God when we flat-out disagree with Him, it might be the greatest opportunity to know and experience God. In unique and impactful ways, He will transform your soul bucket and refine it like gold in fire.

Let's be honest. How often haven't we thought something would make us happy only to go after it, put it in our soul bucket, and be disappointed or disenchanted? The happiness you are chasing after is not what you think it is and will not satisfy you. These things we are chasing after are temporary and circumstantial.

I know that death to self sounds drastic and dramatic, and you may think, *I did not sign up for this.* But before you close this book, I want you to know I felt the same way.

VANESA ALCANTARA

I was not entirely sure what I signed up for when I began working on my soul bucket. None of us want to hear that we must die to live a joy-filled life. But the reality is this: If you follow Christ, dying to self in order to live is our greatest lesson. His example of living was laying His life down for others and dying to Himself so that we might truly live!

When we step away from the self-sacrificing nature of the Christian walk and our call to embody the love and power of Christ in the world, we settle for counterfeits that produce selfishness and a life devoid of the Spirit of God. If you create a life where you don't need help, faith, hope, objective truth, direction, conviction, or divine comfort, what place does the Holy Spirit have in your life? And what are you producing with your life?

My sister, I have come to you today to interrupt the cycle and implore you to take a hard look at your life. Ask yourself the question:

What kind of "water" am I drinking?

Psalms 26:2 NIV says,

Test me, Lord, and try me, examine my heart and my mind;

Ask yourself, "What is spilling out of me? Is love, compassion, and patience flowing out of me? Is empowerment by the Holy Spirit spilling out of me? Am I compelled to go and do what God has called me to do—is purpose coming out of me?

Whether you realize it or not, what's inside you, spills out from you. Examine your soul bucket. You may be surprised by what you find.

Heavenly Father, only You know what is really in our soul buckets. You know what needs to go, you know what I need even when I can't put my finger on it. Continue the work You've started. In Jesus' Name, amen.

Chapter 2 Challenge: Reflect & Redirect

Reflect on these Scriptures and say these out loud. The Word of God is life, so fill your soul bucket with it.

> *I have been crucified with Christ. It is no longer I who live, but Christ who lives in me. And the life I now live in the flesh, I live by faith in the Son of God, who loved me and gave himself for me.* Galatians 2:20 ESV

> *For whoever would save his life will lose it, but whoever loses his life for my sake and the gospel's will save it.* Mark 8:35 ESV

And he said to all, 'If anyone would come after me, let him deny himself and take up his cross daily and follow me. Luke 9:23 ESV.

Ask yourself these tough questions:

What am I turning to instead of Jesus? What people or resources seem to be more reliable than God? In what ways do they cause me harm? Create a plan to let these go.

_____
_____
_____
_____
_____
_____
_____
_____
_____
_____
_____
_____
_____
_____
_____
_____
_____
_____

The Wells We Turn To

WHERE WE GO INSTEAD OF JESUS

"YOU WILL ONLY TASTE TRUE FREEDOM WHEN YOU DRINK FROM THE LIVING WELL." – VANESA ALCANTARA

October of 2021 was the year I turned 33 and was also the year my life got twisted upside down. Sitting in my friend's car, I reflected on why it was such a significant year.

Passionately, I expressed, "At 33 years of age, Jesus, the son of God, gave up his life for us! And Just as He gave up His life, I want to do the same. I want God to break me for His glory. I want to die in all the areas where he wants me to die."

Whoa! It was such a profound reflection that I even posted it on my social media for all to see and be inspired to do the same. To die to self so that we may truly live. It resonated so deeply for me.

Two weeks later, my body reacted to post-covid symptoms that woke up all sorts of health issues and dysfunctions in my body and brain. Life felt like it had been snatched away from me. I lost my ability to walk, and the fine motor skills in my dominant right hand were gone. I vividly remember trying to walk, but my feet wouldn't work. Neuropathy had taken over my extremities, killing off connections in my nervous system. When I tried to walk, my feet felt like glass pierced through my skin with every step. It was excruciating. Days would come and go where I barely moved. It was significant for me to make it from the couch to the bed and back. This painful existence became my new routine *for months*.

I will never forget my kids' faces when they asked, "Mommy, when are you going to get better?" My husband did everything he could in our home while wondering if his wife would make it and if he was on his way to becoming a widowed dad. All the physical and emotional pain put tremendous pressure on my family and weighed down my soul buckets in ways I could have never imagined, let alone anticipated! Despair and hopelessness filled the air in our home. Sadness and depression seemed to join us in bed as they made themselves at home. My family carried this burden as a whole, and it was disheartening. Waiting on the Lord felt too painful, and it became so easy to allow anger to fill my soul. I didn't want to deal with this! I was tired. I felt so done.

Have you been there?

Feelings of uselessness and disappointment slowly led me into a living pit of despair, depression, and anger. Though I wanted to return to 100%, my body insisted on staying put (at what felt like 2%). One would think a good Christian woman like me would fill her time with sermons, uplifting worship music, and dedicate time reading the Word!

But that was not the case at all.

Like many of us, I vegged out, numbed myself, and filled my soul buckets with streaming services, bringing counterfeit "comfort" and distraction. Anger caused me to believe several narratives that were untrue. I was sure God had let me down. At times I even questioned my faith, not the kind where I'm not sure if I believed in Jesus, the kind where it took faith to accept He had my best interest at heart.

Faith said, "God will heal you, even if it's not on this side of heaven." Faith encouraged me to hang onto the Truth that He had never left me, that He was sitting in pain with me, holding me. If there was a faith bucket inside me, that bucket was bone dry and nailed upside down.

My issues of emotional abandonment had resurfaced. Every time I prayed, I begged, "Lord, please!! This time, can you lessen my pain so I can sleep? Please. It's been too many days without sleep..."

The response felt non-existent.

I would wait, feeling the warmth of my tears on my face as I lay there waiting. Nothing would happen. A rush of profound disappointment would overtake me, not only because He didn't answer me like I hoped He would, but because of *my lack of faith*. I knew who He was before this infirmity entered my body. I knew Him to be a healer, a bondage breaker, a miracle worker, a promise keeper, a faithful Father, a good God, a mighty warrior, and a strong tower. All these truths would flood my mind, but they felt so far from my reality.

I now know that God was trying to teach me that feelings are horrible masters. And regardless of my circumstances or emotions, the slightest bit of faith can revolutionize a mindset.

Faith, the size of a mustard seed, was an option I pushed away while trying to fill my soul bucket from other cisterns. My anger towards God created feelings of abandonment, depression, and despair led me to seek other wells for comfort to distract me from my soul's reality.

When we turn to other wells of life to fill us, we will quickly realize the high of "fulfillment" is temporary. Not only that, the hit does not last long. We find that turning back to the true Well of Life is our only option to finding health and wholeness in Christ. Towards the end of this chapter, we will walk through how to do this practically.

Here are a few examples of wells that we humans turn to. and how each one deeply impacts us.

The Well of Comfort

We live in a society that preaches, "Do what makes you feel good!" Marketing companies and social media platforms tell us that if we do what makes us feel good, we will ultimately gain all that we've ever wanted—happiness.

Fast food and car commercials are infamous for this.

They can market a burger so well it makes you believe that if you have that burger, you can have the same satisfaction they're promoting. They'll make you think your life will be filled with smiles, sunny skies, and romance if you drink a cold soda! Girl, even these allergy commercials have become next level. I don't even have allergies, but these happy twirling commercial people made me want to stock up on some allergy medication!

The message of most well-marketed products seems to be, "This product (whatever it is) can immediately satisfy your desire and make you feel great." It's no wonder I turned to food in my darkest moments! My daily dose of excruciating pain demanded instant relief, but relief was nowhere to be found. Since none of my medications provided the comfort I craved, I turned to the easiest temporary solution: food.

I decided I would eat my little heart out.

I would have all the chips and snacks I wanted, because I felt sad, angry and deserving of comfort. Though I was physically harming my body this way, it gave me a false sense of relief. While distracting myself with food, I failed to realize that my soul was starving—not for chips, but for a solid and reliable source of comfort. Often, we can become so fixated on pursuing comfort through external avenues that we neglect the equally powerful craving our soul experiences amidst our pain. The comfort we often need is supernatural.

We become *so* self-centered when we turn to our own devices for comfort. God is removed from the equation when our quest to feel better starts and ends with us. But when we turn to God for comfort, He gives us eyes to see purpose in our pain.

2 Corinthians 1:3-4 NIV says,

> *Praise be to the God and Father of our Lord Jesus Christ, the Father of compassion and the God of all comfort, who comforts us in all our troubles, so that we can comfort those in any trouble with the comfort we receive from God.*

When we go to a false well of comfort, we have nothing to give to the people around us. A bag of chips did not help me or my sisters (who were around me). But when we go to the Father of ALL comfort, He comforts us in such a way that we become bearers of His comfort, able to comfort those around us who are also hurting. Often God uses those moments to show us that life is about more than just us. The pain you are experiencing is temporary, but the Bread of Life is eternal. Turn to God for comfort. Watch how HE will give you tools to have, use, and invite others to feast on.

The Well of Control

When we are desperate, we will try to do anything in our power to keep things afloat in all areas of our life. When things go "under," we can feel a sense of failure, so we work hard to avoid this uncomfortable feeling at all costs. We try to do this by taking control.

Taking control of a situation can be helpful, especially when we are in fight-or-flight mode and have to quickly access this part of our brain to protect ourselves from pain or danger. I saw this play out in my dark season as I fought to regain control over my life. Because God's answers were not coming quickly enough for me, Google became my source of understanding. *Google, what's going on with me? My hands don't work. My feet don't work. What disease do I have, Google?*

We all have had our 'Dear Google' moments, hoping to find answers that would put us back in the driver's seat of our lives. As we turn to this well of control, we turn our backs on the truth that He is a good father, regardless of how utterly chaotic our lives feel. Where control gives us the illusion that we can determine the desired results, control becomes our source and, over time, becomes an idol in our lives. More often than not, if we are honest with ourselves, we don't believe God will come through for us so we anxiously strive, working hard to protect ourselves from feeling the pain that could overtake us.

The well of control is filled to the top with fear. You must be careful! If we aren't careful, fear can become lord over our lives. As before, emotions are horrible masters.

> *No man can serve two masters: for either he will hate the one and love the other, or else he will hold to the one and despise the other.*
> Matthew 6:24-26 (KJV)

The more you go to the well of control, the more your soul bucket fills with it, causing your heart to hold onto the wrong master. You can choose to love or to hate. Choose what to let go of and what to hold onto. If fear drives you to the well of control, I challenge you with this; grab fear by the neck and bring it to the well of Perfect Love.

1 John 4:18 ESV says,

> *There is no fear in love, but perfect love casts out fear. For fear has to do with punishment, and whoever fears has not been perfected in love.*

The Well of Distraction

This one is a doozy and probably the devil's most successful weapon.

Have you ever binged so many shows to distract yourself that the characters in the shows became your best friends? As entertaining as these things can be, they can be addicting, intoxicating, and distracting.

Life would tell me that the physical pain I was in kept me from being able to deal with emotional distress. I felt like I had no time for emotional work because the physical pain kept me from my everyday life. But here's the gag. Whenever there *was* potential time and space to deal with it, I sabotaged it by distracting myself with something mindless.

One of my favorite escapes was browsing and daydreaming on Zillow. We had just bought our house the year prior! I distracted myself with the possibility of starting over. That would change everything, right? What was I thinking?!

Sis, why can't we be content? Why are we so prone to run away from our challenges instead of facing them head-on? You have a much higher chance of gaining victory by dealing and healing than you ever will by ignoring and scrolling.

I can't help but think of the story of Jonah in the Bible. He is an excellent example of what it looks like when we cling to our wells instead of trusting God with the unknown. God gave Jonah instructions that would put him in an uncomfortable position. But this position would bear the fruit of setting so many people free. Unfortunately, Jonah tried to control his circumstance by running away and ended up in a dark place far away from God's plan. Feel free to read the book of Jonah, where you will find more, but I want to highlight just a short section.

Jonah 1:1-3 NIV says:

> *1The word of the Lord came to Jonah son of Amittai: 2"Go to the great city of Nineveh and preach against it, because its wickedness has come up before me." 3But Jonah ran away from the Lord and headed for Tarshish. He went down to Joppa, where he found a ship bound for that port. After paying the fare, he went aboard and sailed for Tarshish to flee from the Lord.*

Like Jonah, many of us have paid the fare. We have boarded ships of fear, anxiety, insecurity, and numbing addictions, not realizing how these boats of comfort, control and distraction can steer us far from God and His call over our lives. Jonah was not thinking about the near future and how it would bring glory to God. Jonah didn't know that on the other side of his obedience, God would use him to lead countless people to Himself.

The same is true for you.

If you read the whole story of Jonah, you find that he got thrown off that ship of distraction, comfort, and control, right into the belly of a fish deep down in the ocean. You know good and well that's a story only God could orchestrate. Jonah lost his way and had no choice but to scan the depths of his soul while literally in the deep.

His mind, will, and emotions needed to be processed by the One who knew him better than he knew himself. That was the only way his soul bucket was getting out of that fish bucket.

I love this quote by Thomas Moore, who wrote *The Dark Night of the Soul.* It says:

> *You are in the belly of the whale to get to Nineveh, to become part of the world, to add your important voice to its song. The people are waiting for you to be offered into Society. They need you, and you need them. But you have to be prepared by your dark night, which is both your pain and your deliverance.*

What are you running away from? Which "ships" have you invested time and energy in with your improperly filled soul buckets? Do you see how they could be causing you to feel trapped in your decisions now?

What are you afraid to face? If you feel stuck, discontented, and in a rut of pain, there is a way out! You don't have to stay there. There is an opportunity to heal, grow, and make a lasting impact in your life and the lives of others. YOU have the power to decide what happens next. However, if you choose to stay the same, you will experience the same—more pain, more frustration, more exhaustion. And not only will that pain inflict you, but it will continue to affect those around you.

Let God help you face it.

By His grace, you will conquer it! Stop being hurled into unnecessary storms because of your fear of the process. God is with you and will sustain you every step of the way!

You may struggle with a deep sadness you've felt for a long time. Perhaps you even hide it from the people closest to you. You tell yourself that no one will be able to help or understand. Then, instead of dealing with it, you do just like Jonah did.

Jonah remembered the closeness he once felt toward God. He had such a closeness that he could hear God give him direct instructions. That only comes from having a genuine relationship with the Lord and actively receiving His love. He remembered the God that loved him and called him by name. He remembered the all-knowing God, the One who is consuming fire and, simultaneously, a strong force of peace and intimate love.

For the record, the One Jonah is talking about is the SAME GOD WHO LOVES YOU. He wants to walk you through your fears and dismantle the lies saying you are worth nothing. And just like Jonah, you can begin to change things with the healing power of your intimacy with Christ, even if you have to go through a similar journey as Jonah.

I know.

I was there through my health journey. Though it took me a minute, I came to the end of myself and said, "You know what? The truth is, I don't know how to take a drink from You. I feel unsafe in this space because I keep asking You for something, and I'm not seeing anything."

That was all He needed from me.

And that's all He wants from you.

He desires your willingness to show up with an open heart, ready for surgery. Even with all the muck and mire in there, allow the REAL Living Water to flood and pressure wash your soul! John 4:14 NIV says,

> *But whoever drinks the water I give them will never thirst. Indeed, the water I give them will become in them a spring of water welling up to eternal life.*

That sounds like a recurring, refreshing wash to my soul.

When Christ is the Lord of our lives, the detours, and distractions in life do not determine the destinies of our souls. Hang on to the only One who can lead you out of these traps and straight into all He has for you.

He is the oasis! Elevate your relationship with God to a true partnership centered around Christlikeness. When you do, your soul will experience the wildest pleasures, the purest joy, the holiest of adventures, and a much deeper sense of fulfillment. In its best form, a life lived for Jesus is a life that demonstrates love through holiness. As we sacrifice the ideas embedded within our soul buckets, we take on the call to die to ourselves in every way necessary. Only then can we learn how to represent Christ in the world correctly. Best of all, the Spirit *empowers* us to do so.

Talk about an energy boost!

And once God fills us, who He is will spill out of our soul buckets; rivers of living water will overflow.

You are probably thinking, *That all makes sense, but what do I do about this mess I'm in right now?* Or, *How do I even do all this? I need practical steps!*

Sis, what you do next will bring life—or death—to your relationship with God. Consider carefully. Your next move will impact the rest. If you want to work on this, you must put your trust in the manufacturer of your soul bucket. Abba-Father is the Designer and Creator of it, not a second or third party.

I know life has not been panning out how you thought it would. But there is hope. You haven't *kicked the bucket* yet, so your life is not over. You'll need to change your perspective and elevate your goals, but the work is worth it. YOU are worth it. Still, the way to get there will be challenging. It will require you to put to death those deep-seated beliefs, habits, and seemingly reliable ways of getting what you want out of life and returning to the mysterious, not-so-controllable relationship that produces life and life more abundantly. You need to trust that God has made His greater joy and fulfillment available to you, exceeding the happiness you can create for yourself. Return to the One who is greater than you. Hit the refresh button. Return to Christ, your first love, the One who will fill your soul bucket to overflow.

At the risk of coming off too "churchy," I want to encourage you to lean into a word that, unfortunately, sounds more and more like vintage Christianity.

That word is **repentance**.

It means turning your back on the earthly soul bucket fillers and facing Jesus, THE Well of Life. Repentance is the act of giving him your dirty soul buckets and allowing Him to turn them over so you can start over. You must avoid sinful actions contrary to God's Word and against whom He has created you to be. Turn your back towards your sin and your face towards Him.

It might be the most challenging yet continual work you will do.

But time and time again, it is worth it. As hard as it might be, you must acknowledge how you've muddied God's purpose for your life by trying to do things as you see fit. Acknowledge how selfishness has gotten in the way. Determine to allow the Word of God to convict you and lead you—not society, family, culture, or even your own longings. Trust God to fulfill you where the world and your efforts cannot.

Sometimes we aren't sure how to approach God or what to say. So, I would love to walk you through a prayer of repentance today.

Let's pray this prayer together:

Heavenly Father, I come to You acknowledging who You are. You are mighty and powerful. Your hands created the Earth and sky, the mighty seas, and your hands have made me. But, Lord, there are ways that I've been living out of line. I've been out of alignment with who You've called me to be. Examine my heart and expose the sin that so easily entangles me. Forgive me for my selfish ways. I've wanted things my way. Help me to please You and bring honor to You with my actions. I lay down my picture of what life should be. I commit to learning from You and ask that You show me Your picture for every aspect of my life. Help me through this, Holy Spirit. I invite You into this process. In Jesus' name, I pray, Amen.

May our fears draw us to the One who can turn our fears into trust. Friend, you will *only* taste true freedom when you drink from the Living Well.

Chapter 3 Challenge: Steps to Making You Well

I want to challenge you to create the space and time to invite Jesus into those wells of your life. And I pray that you will be open and allow your soul bucket to be ready to receive from your Heavenly Father.

Take a few minutes to do the following exercise:

1. Write down some new habits you can create in place of habits that are not serving you?

2. Write an encouraging note to your future self. What do you want to remind yourself of a year from now? Five years? Next week? What is something you hope to overcome?

Lord, help the walls to come down as this reader sits in Your presence. Search her heart and help her learn more about who You are in her circumstances. In Jesus' name. Amen.

_____

_____

_____

_____

_____

_____

_____

_____

_____

_____

_____

_____

VANESA ALCANTARA

VANESA ALCANTARA

4

Healing From Disguises

SURRENDERING COUNTERFEIT STRENGTH

"DOES OUR PICTURE OF TRUE STRENGTH MATCH GOD'S ORIGINAL DESIGN?"
– VANESA ALCANTARA

Without Jesus, the living well, we cannot heal our soul's diseases or resist the false safety of our distractions. Yet so many of us stay stuck. We know the internal work needs to happen, but we hide in shame. Rather than dealing, we hide and protect ourselves with disguises. This tendency to hide goes back to Adam and Eve and the soul scanning they didn't do.

After discovering they were naked, they hid from God and manufactured fig leaf coverings. Shame caused them to cover up their vulnerabilities instead of being open with God and allowing Him to help them through it.

We all have emotional and mental baggage we need to sort through.

We often need to enlist the help of someone else, but we don't. The embarrassment and shame keep our souls heavy-laden. The burden of it all becomes a heavy mask or a type of suit we put on. We suffer in this apparel while underneath, the weight of our disguises crushes our weary souls.

Throughout the years, I've learned that it takes more courage to be honest with ourselves about our current emotional and mental state, than to be honest with "Jo Shmo" from down the street. The masks and suits we put on can initially feel like such strength. But it is a strength laced with deception and is also very unsustainable.

"Wow, no one will ever know all I'm going through," you tell yourself. "You keep it together very well."

Sis, that is the lying voice of false strength that tells us,

"We push through. That's what we strong independent women do!" Or,

"It runs in my family! Strong women don't give in to weakness." Or,

"We move forward no matter what."

All of these may seem very bold, courageous, and even admirable, but there is a narrative underneath this that breaks my heart. It's the narrative that says, "My pain is an obstacle I must jump over and not a wound worth tending to."

Counterfeit Strength

I grew up around feisty Latina women who came to the United States hoping for progress and a better life. Even though they didn't all grow up in America, I found that society's messages and false promises could still easily infiltrate their hurting hearts. These women came from their country, feeling pressured to demonstrate strength and courage, which they learned through their early pains and childhood experiences. They came to the United States with hearts full of old hurts and new dreams of creating a different reality.

But the only language they knew was *survival*. Carry on at all costs. Work hard, survive, and give your children a better chance at life.

I often eavesdropped as the women in my family created kitchen cleaning therapy sessions. I could hear the pain in their voices as they vented about how tiring it was to put up with men. Yet, they stuck together, and in protective lioness fashion, they prayed passionately and fiercely for their men and family circumstances. They urged each other not to allow things to continue as they were and to do what they had to do to push through and keep going. As they tried to make sense of things, they would point out all the warning signs they should have learned from and acted on in the past.

Sometimes you couldn't tell if they were scolding or encouraging each other. Still, they always committed to praying and reminding each other that they could pull through. In some ways, I saw so much beauty in the community aspect of these kitchen therapy sessions. It was easy to become enamored with their care and even convinced that the women in my family were right to have their fiery anger!

Often the conversations would deepen. Sometimes, while the men's coffee was brewing on the stove, the women would explore their childhood traumas, seeking a way to deal so they could some-how heal from it all but never knowing how. My family would relate to one another as the ladies processed out loud. I remember how the room would shift when one of them suddenly squared up, one hand on their hip and the other up in the air with their finger pointed sternly. It was a kind of power pose, reminding the other women *not* to be passive or dependent on men. It was a physical cue to be strong and resilient as a woman.

But it also demanded they trust the Lord, even when facing their darkest sorrows.

Whether I realized it or not, I was taking mental notes like a faithful student. I was learning the survival skills of a neglected, traumatized tribe who lacked the tools to express the raw truth in their hearts. They didn't know how to look their men in the eyes and speak vulnerably about their actual fears and desires.

Yet, behind their cloudy eyes, I could hear their hearts cry.

Hurting Heart Cries

If I could put words to their aching pain that was disguised with counterfeit strength, I think their hearts would be saying:

I feel sad that our life has turned out so hard.
I feel anxious that we won't be able to pay our rent.
I'm sad because our fridge is empty, and I don't know what to cook.
I'm so exhausted and can't ask for help.
I feel like you've emotionally abandoned me.
I'm scared to complain because you work so hard for our family.
So, instead I bicker, because I don't want you to see my fears.
Have you lost interest because I've gained weight?
I feel scared that you're hiding something from me.
I feel scared that you're cheating on me...again.
I feel angry because I feel alone.

When you don't have the tools or the personal confidence to express your heart, especially during times of chaos, you survive by disguising your fears in counterfeit strength. It's kind of like filling your soul buckets from the wrong wells, but it goes deeper. This trusted disguise that far too often gets passed down from generation to generation of women causes us to show up in the world incorrectly.

Maybe, like me, you've noticed the same things growing up. You saw the family norms and patterns and perhaps even vowed never to be the kind of woman who demeaned men in her anger. But what if you've never learned how to live life differently? Maybe you, too, got sucked into the cycle because somewhere along the line, you bought into the lie that tells us, "This is what strong women look like."

We appear as powerful women who create our security for ourselves, proudly succeeding without the help of men. If you've ever been a woman in pain, I'm sure you've received some version of this same "Strong Woman" advice. As empowering and supportive as it might seem to receive such passionate advice from other women, I want us to stop and ask ourselves,

What was God's original design for women?

Does our picture of true strength match God's original design?

When we look closely at the inner workings of real families and their "strong" women, we realize that the power they often put forth does not demonstrate a desirable strength. Rather, it reveals the painful cross women feel forced to carry. Their feminine power does not come from an overflow of confidence and relational flourishing. They are strong because they must be, not because they are well nurtured and spilling over.

Society will say that strong women are women who create security for themselves. They voice their opinions, thoughts, and requests as they see fit and according to what they feel, without regard or thought on how men receive their words. After all, we are wiser and more prepared to define truth and fairness. And in the process, women grow cold and unwilling to put up with the seeming incompetence of men. We demand emotional maturity, emotional generosity, and emotional reciprocation. And in our frustration, we use passive-aggressive tactics to keep men accountable. We use manipulation disguised as women's intuition and call it wisdom, but we deceive ourselves.

In our tired and angry state, we consume entertainment with our guard down (remember the Well of Distraction?). And unknowingly, the media becomes our teacher and master. We learn to use our feminine strength, not to partner with the men in our lives, but to make up for their shortcomings. Even when men are willing and capable, some women choose their own strength because it seems better, more consistent, and more reliable.

The media constantly bombards us with this imagery that teaches women to see sensuality and control as their superpower. Our children's shows are no exception. No kid's show is complete without the wise, responsible mom paired with the ridiculous, idiotic dad. Even the siblings on TV have a similar dynamic. Protective, responsible brothers have been replaced by sassy, entitled big sisters who must put up with the annoying immaturity of their little brothers. And we laugh at the punchlines as if the media reflects our family experiences.

Is that true, though?

We have found it easier to accept society's incomplete, feminist solution to our relational brokenness. Culture has done a great job of persuading us to control our relationships rather than working to identify our deepest fears, wounds, and longings and dealing with them so we can heal and grow from them.

Have we forgotten the art of hard conversations and vulnerability? Has society influenced your ideas of how real strength can look?

We must guard our hearts against these dangers. If Society's messaging goes unchecked, never passing through the filter of Biblical truth, its false messages will inevitably seep into the soul buckets of our daily lives.

Unfortunately, so many of us are trying to assemble the puzzle pieces of life without having the reference picture on the box.

If we were to pull back the curtain of our hearts, we would see our human effort for what it is. Hopefully, we can realize our thoughts are not the same as God's for how a woman can win in her life. Our faulty human response to pain is to buy into the lie that says we must stop depending on men to demonstrate strength as women.

Does any of this sound familiar?

Yup.

I know these thoughts too well because they were mine, too.

Friend, I hate to break it to you, but this layer of disguise is called *pride*!

Pride offers false protection from the instability that we fear. Our tender hearts get lost in protective arrogance and the need for control. But we puff up with pride because we have unresolved fear. The most significant area where this pride shows up is our relationships.

Here is how the hardened heart gets built: fears and unmet expectations get a protective layer of pride. Whenever we get hurt or don't do the soul-work of being honest with ourselves, we add another layer to protect, mask or disguise what is really there. Before we know it, our pride begins dismantling other people in our lives, piece by piece. We criticize their every move without caring for that person's emotional or mental state because our heart gets buried under thick layers of deep hurt.

The old saying is true, *hurt people hurt people.*

But rather than seeing the effects of this emotional (and spiritual) war tactic, family units in so many parts of the world celebrate this "strong independent woman" profile as a sign of progress and personal advancement. But when you eavesdrop on these kitchen venting sessions, you realize "girl power" can sometimes be misleading. True inner strength is often nowhere to be found, and this counterfeit version leaves us sad, lonely, and tired.

So how do we develop true strength?

The answer is Christ.

He is the True Help.

Ezer

Abiding in Christ gives you the tools to live out your God-given design. Scriptures say that when He created Eve, He created an *ezer*.

Ezer is a Hebrew word usually translated as "help" or "helper" in the Bible. You might have heard it used about women. However, looking at the word more closely, we see God as the most essential *ezer* in the Bible. We can glean its beautiful meaning for women only by understanding how this word describes God. Genesis 2:18 (ESV) says:

> *Then the LORD God said, "It is not good that the man should be alone; I will make him a helper fit for him."*

This word helper shows up twenty-one times. Two out of the twenty-one are in reference to women. But the nineteen other times refer to our Lord God! Most of these verses reference how God is the *ezer* of His people and how He helps Israel defeat its enemies.[1]

Here is an example:

> *And this he said of Judah: "Hear, O LORD, the voice of Judah, and bring him in to his people. With your hands contend for him, and be a help against his adversaries."*
> Deuteronomy 33:7 (ESV)

We learn in Scripture that God made us in His image. Both men and women.

> *So God created mankind in his own image, in the image of God he created them; male and female he created them.* Genesis 1:27-28 (ESV)

---

1. https://www.theologyofwork.org/key-topics/women-and-work-in-th e-old-testament/god-created-woman-as-an-ezer-kind-of-helper-gen esis-218#

Ezer as an attribute also used for God is mind-blowing! Woven into our very DNA is a *strength* that flows not from our human effort but from God Himself. God's strength and power caused the raging seas to be calm. His help would bring Daniel out of a lion's den with zero injuries. God's help would cause enemies to be swallowed by the waters' depths when Israelites crossed the Red Sea. We can see God's help and strength when He caused the walls of Jericho to come down. The walls collapsed by the sheer power of God. The power of God is supernatural, beyond our comprehension.[2]

He is True Strength. And that SAME power *lives inside of you.* Your femininity is beautiful, flexible, yet strong. You were made with tremendous ability to build, tear down, create, procreate, and impact others in more ways than you know!

The woman described in Proverbs 31 has all the following qualities (from ESV):

- Trustworthy (31:11)

- Hardworking (31:13)

- Cares for others (31:15)

- Strong (31:17)

- Generous (31:20)

- Well-prepared (31:21)

- Dignified (31:25)

- Wise and kind (31:26)

- Industrious (31:27)

- Fears the Lord (31:30)

---

2. From Psalms 18:13–15; Daniel 4:35; Job 38:4–6

Culture and society have tried to diminish the word help, but do not succumb to the ways of this world by thinking this way.

Sis. God, *YAHWEH* is *Ezer* as well. Through His fingertips, you were etched, carved, and molded together. Through His stripes, you were forgiven and healed. Through His help and strength, God has empowered you to go out into the world and be a living witness to what He can do in and through you.

You are a miracle.
The things you have gone through for some have torn them apart.
For others, their life has felt like a gift from the start. For some, their pain causes them to believe God has cursed them. God, who is all-powerful, who is true strength, the One who sees you in your truest form wants you whole. It's His True Strength, met with your weaknesses that give you the real strength that helps you to deal, heal, and grow.

I encourage you to love yourself enough to bring all of your disguises and weaknesses to the feet of Jesus. Admit that these dis- guises keep you from loving yourself and others well. Allow God's healing to flow and discover your ability to stand in actual strength today!

Let's pray about it:

Heavenly Father, I pray for my sister right now. The person reading this book is Your incredible creation. I pray, in the name of Jesus, that she would lay down all her disguises before You, Lord. You know them all, and You know them well. All the ways she has suited up in her human strength and put aside Your armor. All the ways she's covered up her pain and remained oblivious to how she is hurting. Expose the lies. Expose the false strength. Help her heart to surrender more fully to You. Help her surrender to Your power. Your Word says that You are our present help in time of need. You will deliver us.

Holy Spirit, move in my sister's heart. Let Your kindness lead her to repentance. I pray that she will stand today in the authority and true strength You have given her to walk in. In the Mighty Name of Jesus, I pray, Amen.

Chapter 4 Challenge: The Disguise of Pride

Journal about the ways pride has shown up in your life. As you strip yourself of pride, what will you put on instead?

_____

_____

_____

_____

_____

_____

_____

_____

_____

_____

_____

_____

_____

_____

_____

_____

_____

_____

_____

_____

_____

_____

Phase II

HEAL FROM IT...
CHAPTERS 5-7

In this next section,
we will address items in
our emotional bag that
need healing or removal.
These are the parts of our
souls that need a touch
from God. In this next
part of the journey, you
will explore strategies
you need to go from
sitting in your pain to
thriving in your purpose.

It's time to heal.

$\mathcal{DIG}$-eases

DO YOU WANT TO BE WELL?

"WHEN WE ACCOMMODATE OUR DYSFUNCTIONS INSTEAD OF DEALING WITH THEM, WE MAKE ALTARS OF OUR ANGER, WOUNDS, AND FEARS."
— VANESA ALCANTARA

In John chapter 5, we find Jerusalem's pool of Bethesda. There are many blind, lame, and paralyzed people gathered at the pool. They believed an angel stirred the water, filling it with healing properties. So, many would lay and wait attentively, hoping not to miss their opportunity to enter the pool when the angel stirred the water. They believed this was their way to be healed. But honestly, the situation created some issues. What if you couldn't see or hear when the waters were being stirred? What if you couldn't move to put yourself inside this pool?!

Because I am a visual person, when I read this story, my brain immediately turns this into a comedy. What could that have been like in real time?

Follow me for a moment.

Let's imagine it was you lying by this pool surrounded by a group of women, and all these women carried a particular issue. Maybe you swat the flies with your good hand as you look around and think to yourself.

How will the one on the left get in if she can't see?

How will the one on the right get in if she can't walk?

How will the lady in front of you get in if she can't move?

Was it impossible for these people to be well? No! Did it take resourcefulness and leaning on each other to make things happen? Yes! They needed to have conversations with one another. They needed collaboration with each other to secure the healing they needed. The man in John 5 was lying on a mat, paralyzed for 38 years. And in all those years, he never asked anyone for a lift into the pool. So, why didn't he get any help? What kept him from getting into the pool of healing?

The day came when Jesus appeared at the place many had called their home. In my imagination, the group are talking amongst themselves at their "hang out" around the pool when Jesus suddenly approaches the scene. And maybe Jesus kneels next to the man before asking him the simple, yet loaded, question.

Jesus asks, "Do you want to be healed?"

Without hesitation, the man looks up at Jesus. "Sir," he says, "I have no one to put me into the pool when the water is stirred up, and while I am going, others step out in front of me."

How we position ourselves when we are in distress makes all the difference.

If it were me, I would have screamed, "YES!" I would have flung my arms up like a baby, signaling Jesus to pick me up and heal me however He saw fit. To be fair, the man at the pool had no idea who

Jesus was yet. He didn't realize that the man who stepped in front of this pool was the Messiah, the Living Water Himself.

Perhaps, after 38 years, he just accepted his life would never be different. In his pain and ignorance, he completely bypassed Jesus' invitation, jumping straight to default excuses. Maybe this man, who remained unnamed, had an idea of how it would all work out. He probably thought someone would bring him into the pool *one day*, and healing would come that way. Or maybe he just accepted that he would die right there by the pool.

Either way, the man lived with no hope in his heart.

But instead of allowing the man to remain stuck in his narrative, Jesus gave him power-filled instructions straight from God. Jesus told him to pick up his mat and walk! When Jesus stepped into the scene, the man faced a choice. Either he could continue to lay on his mat, making excuses for himself, or he could answer the question. Matter of fact, Sis, you may need ask yourself some similar questions right now. Be honest with yourself.

Have you given up?

Have you tried to pursue change for years and seen no result, day after day?

Have you just accepted that your life is what it is?

Who or what are you waiting on to help you heal, deal, and grow?

When we accommodate our dysfunctions instead of dealing with them, we make altars of our anger, wounds, and fears. But when we reposition ourselves to face Jesus, we encounter the Healer who knows us best! Our Savior can tend to our wounds in ways that bring healing and freedom. It's what he came to do!

> *The Spirit of the Lord God is upon me, Because the Lord has anointed and commissioned me To bring good news to the humble and afflicted; He has sent me to bind up [the wounds of] the brokenhearted, To proclaim release [from confinement and condemnation] to the [physical*

and spiritual] captives And freedom to prisoners. Isaiah 61:1 AMP

I believe it all comes down to the posture we take. The man at the well could have accepted that his strategy did not work and chose to listen to what Jesus said about his situation. Think of it as the same choice God is confronting you with *right now*. And let's be real for a moment. You may not believe you need to answer this question. You may be thinking, *I've got things to work on, but I don't have a full-on emotional 'disease.'*

If that is the case, I'd like you to look at it this way. Webster's Dictionary defines this word "disease" as a lack of ease; lack of convenience.

Dis- is the "lack of something."

Ease- is the "Freedom from difficulty, hardship, concern, or anxiety."

How does Dis-ease or LACK of FREEDOM show up in your life?

- *Lack of peace?*

- *Lack of forgiveness?*

- *Lack of self-esteem?*

- *Lack of joy?*

- *Lack of fulfillment?*

- *Lack of self-control?*

Are you willing to do whatever it takes to step into the healing God has made available to you? Or will you continue to lay on a mat of past hurts, lies, unforgiveness, betrayal, or abuse?

Maybe you're the blind one by the pool today. Perhaps you can't see what God has for you. Or perhaps you're the lame one by the pool. You may feel like you keep watching other people move quickly into their best life. You resent how others seem to jump so quickly into new relationships, new opportunities, and different levels of healing while you seem to lag. Rather than thriving, you find yourself limping and dragging yourself through life—just trying to survive. Maybe you feel paralyzed by stress, negative mindsets, and unhealthy loops of coping in ways you know are terrible for you.

We all have internal dis-eases that have kept us from the healing God has made available to us at one point or another.

Will you remain in your brokenness and dysfunction, or will you admit that your default methods do not work and say yes to healing? My sister, I urge you to follow Jesus' instructions. Get up and walk! Receive the healing Jesus is offering you today.

Chapter 5 Challenge: Answer the Question

I want you to think about where you currently stand mentally, emotionally, and physically. What position do you find yourself in? The position you are currently facing will determine your soul's healing, just like those who sat near the pool of Bethesda. Jesus is entering the scene of your life, and He's asking you the same question today. "Do you want to get well?"

Take some time to write about your time at the pool. Don't hold back. Tell the Lord *exactly* what it is you are dealing with in your own words.

In the next chapter, we will talk more in-depth about how to ultimately pick up your mat and walk!

_____
_____
_____
_____
_____
_____
_____
_____
_____
_____
_____
_____
_____
_____
_____
_____

_____

_____

_____

_____

_____

_____

_____

_____

_____

_____

_____

_____

_____

_____

_____

_____

_____

_____

_____

_____

_____

_____

_____

_____

_____

_____

_____

_____

VANESA ALCANTARA

VANESA ALCANTARA

X-rays of the Soul

SOUL SCANNING FOR THE FIRST TIME

I CONSIDER THAT OUR PRESENT SUFFERINGS ARE NOT WORTH COMPARING WITH THE GLORY THAT WILL BE REVEALED IN US. FOR THE CREATION WAITS IN EAGER EXPECTATION FOR THE CHILDREN OF GOD TO BE REVEALED.
ROMANS 8:18-19 NIV

Growing up, I remember hearing stories about God being our Healer, but I was never clear on what healing could look like for me. Instead of trying to give God my unwell soul, I decided it might be easier to put all my efforts into forgetting about my pain. If God could help me forget, maybe that was the way I could be healed.

So, I made myself numb to it, figuring I would no longer feel shame about it if there was "nothing there." It wasn't until my first year of marriage that all the pain I was carrying began bubbling up like a pot of hot milk. The things I fought so hard to keep in low heat began popping up in my life. The situation left me no choice but to step into the un-comfortability of the heat in order to heal.

I had to face the things keeping me from accessing my healing. And my healing was waiting, ready and available to me. There was a darkness in my soul I knew Jesus wanted to free me from, and all I needed was the faith of a mustard seed.

That's all you need too!

There is a step of faith the man by the pool of Bethesda took that we can all take as well. Learning how to scan our souls through the filter of God's Word is crucial to achieve the goal of *dealing* with it.

I remember one day asking God to scan my soul and help me identify the dis-eases that were keeping me stuck. In a time of prayer, I received this mental picture of a chest x-ray filled with dark spots. The chest represented the soul and each dark spot symbolized the unhealed wounds I had been carrying for a long time.

I had been...

- Suffocated by secrets

- Blinded by the enemy's lies

- Paralyzed by fear of rejection

- Crippled by sinful patterns

- Stained by fornication and perversion

- Silenced by sexual abuse

This is when the Lord birthed the phrase Soul Scan in me. It was in a time of solitude and reflection where I was able to see what keeps many of us from breakthrough and healing. Impregnated with a vision, I knew God had given me something powerful to lead women closer to Himself. Though there were many times I wanted to quit, I knew I wanted to be *healed* more than I wanted to be *sick*. I was able to see how our ailments keep us bound by the "mats" in our liveslives, convincing us that we will lay there forever. I wanted to point out two mats we become stuck on and how they point to the dark spots in our souls that make us sick.

SECRETS

I remember the first time I went soul-scanning. I was going to professional counseling. The intention was to deal with untouched pain of abuse. I had a plan and a vision of how to repair the brokenness in my life. However, the more the therapist and I excavated my heart and soul, the more I was able to see how my childhood wounds had infected so many parts of my life. When I started to process and allow God to define health for me, I began to see not only significant changes, but also how comfortable I had been on my *mat* all those years. The *mat* I'm referring to is the comfort I found in secrecy. Just as I learned to hide the pain, fears, and sadness, inevitably the joys, dreams, and aspirations were hidden as well. My mat became my *safe place* and my shield that kept rejection at bay.

As the Lord scanned my soul during that healing season, I began to peel back the layers of trauma from years prior. The remaining parts of my unhealed pain were actively shaping how I viewed God, myself, and those around me. It's like a centipede you'd step on to try and kill, only to realize half of it is still moving and twitching. That is how undealt with pain can show up.

The age of six was filled with confusion and trauma for me. Sexual abuse stained me like a leaking pen blotching a white skirt.

Years later, that hurt lead me to medicate through promiscuity, creating a disease of perversion in my life. Instead of Christ becoming my healing the mat became my life vest. Crippled by shame and fear, the mat of secrecy temporarily provided a false sense of security and stability when I needed it the most.

But I didn't know I was still hurting, still horribly wounded.

IGNORANCE

Ignorance is the lack of knowledge or information. I believe we become comfortable in not knowing about a thing if the *thing* will bring us any type of discomfort or pain. We move along through life, pretending our past no longer affects us. We convince ourselves that our current thinking, feeling and actions are unaffected by the past pain. We become comfortable in the unknown because we've always feared uncovering what was really there. Many times, we can feel that something is wrong, but we tell ourselves that the less we know, the better. We agree with notions that say, *ignorance is bliss, unawareness brings contentment, out of sight, out of mind...*

Friend, if that is you, then ignorance has become the *mat* you've been laying on for years.

You are being blinded by the enemy keeping you from seeing what is really there. Scripture says in Proverbs 18:15 ESV,

> *An intelligent heart acquires knowledge, and the ear of the wise seeks knowledge.*

There is so much God wants to reveal to you about Himself and about your heart. There are things you need to repent of, not just for your sake, but to attain keys that will set others free. Before you unlock a door you need a key, before you get the key, you have to *see* where the key sits. Before you see where the key is, you must *know* what door you need to get through and what you hope is on the other side! It is clear why the enemy wants to keep you blinded to your pain. It's because he knows we are powerful when we stand in the truth of who we are. When you seek, the devil knows *you will find*. It's time to get yourself up from that mat and walk. Walk your little tail right to His Word where keys of freedom await!

"Then you will know the truth, and the truth will set you free," says John 8:32 NIV.

It's time to rise up!

DARK SPOTS OF THE SOUL

What dark spots have become diseases in your soul? Here are a few spots that start off as small dots but end up blotting the light all the way out if we don't deal to heal and grow from it.

COMPARISON & JEALOUSY

The seed of comparison starts off very innocently at first. Often it begins with us looking outwardly for inspiration. This can be a good (even a great) thing! But if we aren't careful, it can lead us to a place where jealousy makes us sick. Looking up to others can be fuel for developing our goals, I'm talking relationship, financial, fitness, and more! We can create exponential results when we get genuinely excited about what God is doing in someone else's life. We can allow our faith to rise, believing God could do the same in us as He did in the person we were watching as they bloomed. That seed of admiration can drive us to greater focus and intentionality.

But here is where this seed starts to morph.

Instead of watering the seed, our God-given desire, with words of life, we allow our pain to do the watering, which spoils the seed. We start to believe that maybe a fulfilling life isn't for us. Hope that once watered the seed is now overtaken by pain and darkness. This is the point when we begin to covet what someone else has and disregard our spouse, the children, the home, the job—you know, all the gifts right in front of us! Bitterness, anger and jealousy begin to cloud our judgement when we compare without God's Word or faith in His work in our lives. That spot in our soul can go from a pure desire to an emotional disease keeping us from experiencing gratitude.

79

HEREDITARY DISEASES

Over the years, I have talked with people whose parents and grand-parents have passed down land or sizable inheritances. Many families pass down generational wealth to secure the financial state of their lineage, which is wise and beautiful! Along those same lines, there are destructive heirlooms that families can unknowingly pass down to us in the spirit realm that many of us are not paying close attention to.

Have you ever considered the patterns of your family?

Does divorce seem to run rampant?

What about adultery, disorders, incest, sexual abuse, untimely death, anger, depression, witchcraft, or addiction?

Is this a coincidence, or could the following scriptural realities be evident in your family?

> *The Lord passed before him and proclaimed, "The Lord, the Lord, a God merciful and gracious, slow to anger, and abounding in steadfast love and faithfulness, 7 keeping steadfast love for thousands, forgiving iniquity and transgression and sin, but who will by no means clear the guilty, visiting the iniquity of the fathers on the children and the children's children, to the third and the fourth generation."* Exodus 34:6-7 ESV

You may have generational dis-eases running through your bloodline that have been the cause of some of these dark spots in your soul. They often show up in your life in ways that are difficult to see unless someone points them out to you. And it isn't anything you've done to bring this onto yourself.

Suppose two parents live in a highly stressful environment plagued with things like danger, poverty, or fear. The woman becomes pregnant and remains in that environment. The survival tools needed to make it in those environments are passed down to the baby. This begins to influence the development of that fetus in more ways than one.

This formation would prepare the growing fetus to face the same environmental conditions as the parents. The mom's blood flows constantly through the fetus. The mother's body will spend up to nine months communicating with the fetus, transferring feelings from thoughts and deep-seated beliefs to her unborn child.

I came across a clip from Dr. Joe Dispenza who said the following:

> *DNA itself can be broken into tiny fragments which hold mental, physical, and cellular "blueprints." Our cells can constantly update with information as we go through life, which can change our DNA or simply be absorbed as part of our genetic heritage to program into our offspring.*

Even natural science confirms generational blessings and curses! As you go throughout your life, the cells in your body store memories and survival mechanisms that you may not even need. Our cells constantly replicate themselves according to the "instructions" found in our DNA. Isn't that crazy?! There may have been some instructions you've received that do not apply to you. It is not your trauma, it is not your fear, pain or burden to carry! You do NOT have to live your life as if you are doomed to divorce because it's "just what happens in your family." You do NOT have to be doomed for poverty, or physical sickness. The generational curse can end with you, but not if you are living as if it can't.

If we bring our hearts and lineage before the Lord and ask Him to cleanse us, forgive us (and those who have gone before us), then ask Him to set us free, He will.

The Lord is slow to anger and abounding in steadfast love, forgiving iniquity and transgression, but he will by no means clear the guilty, visiting the iniquity of the fathers on the children to the third and the fourth generation.[1]

The more we keep our brokenness hidden in the dark, untouched by Jesus, the more we risk passing down hereditary diseases through our bloodline. Instead of hiding, let yourself fall apart in Jesus' arms. Let yourself break open. It's time to heal.

Allow Jesus to mend your broken pieces, even the ones no one knows about.

One day, you may be sitting across from someone with a story similar to yours. Do the work of surrendering every part of your life to Jesus, even the unseen, so that when the day comes, you become the vessel of healing. The Lord can use the worst of your life's story to impart the greatest blessing of wisdom to those hurting around you and help lead them to healing in Christ.

DEPRESSION

Depression is an issue running rampant in our culture right now. It's like a bad friend who somehow continues to insert themself in your life, whether you care to have them there or not. Have you ever had someone like this in your life? Someone you know is toxic and needs to be excommunicated from your circle. But somehow, you (and I) let them come around from time to time because we get sucked in by their sob story. We then feel trapped in their cycle of deep sadness which becomes more than their story; it becomes their identity. That's how I see depression, deep sadness that constantly overstays its welcome. It's a real thing that sometimes people cannot fight on their own and because of that, they end up needing assistance. Sometimes assistance looks like talking to a friend, a counselor, or even medication. It's different for everyone, but God is still on the throne of your situation.

---

1. Deuteronomy 5:9

I know that depression has been a dark spot in my own soul throughout the years. It's one I've had to keep in check constantly. The more I keep up with Jesus, the Great Physician, the more I can tell when depression spots are popping back up. Routinely checking in with myself (and with Jesus) is the rhythm I've needed to keep from regressing. When I am not abiding in His word, my spirit grows weak. And when tough times come and depression comes knocking at my door, I get sucked back in more easily.

Here is a great reminder we can speak over ourselves when we are overcome by depression:

> *I waited patiently for the Lord; he turned to me and heard my cry. He lifted me out of the slimy pit, out of the mud and mire; he set my feet on a rock and gave me a firm place to stand. He put a new song in my mouth, a hymn of praise to our God. Many will see and fear the Lord and put their trust in him.* Psalm 40:1-3 NIV

ANXIETY

The year Covid-19 was in full swing around the world; we were all hit with devastation in my house. Not only did I get the virus but, right beforehand, I came down with something that some people live with every day.

Anxiety.

During this time, I experienced my very first panic attack. My body could not handle feeling trapped in a home with my five-month-old baby, a toddler, our 8-year-old daughter, plus the weight of family life. To say I was overwhelmed is an understatement. Like many of you, the unknown, the questions, the stress, the loss, the pain, and the anger most of us experienced led us into waters no one should navigate alone. One night, I found myself on a cold finished basement floor curled up in a ball. I was incapable of moving, but I cried out to God. I had no other place to run to but Him Because I thought this was the end of me.

But God!

Anxiety functions like a disease threatening to end our life. It's a bully, lying to our face. It tells us that we have arrived at the end of ourselves with no way out. Anxiety has bullied us women, causing us to have a fearful heart crippling our soul, for far too long. But enough is enough! Through Christ, you can work through your biggest fears. Healing and freedom *is* for you. And it is for *today!*

Christ came and died on a cross to take on the weight of what keeps in in fear. Though you may find yourself in a season that feels like a dark cold basement with no way out, I'm here to tell you Christ has come so that you may have life. He is fully prepared to pull you out from the pit and turn your mess into a message.

Chapter 6 Challenge: Bring your Dis-eases to Jesus

For this challenge, choose three dis-eases (on the next page) that you will actively combat. Circle the symptoms on the following page that you have felt may point to dis-eases you need God to heal. Take some time with Jesus and ask Him to reveal His heart to you concerning the areas you identified. Ask Him to heal you and give you a new perspective. Write down what He says to your heart. Then, get some accountability on what your plan will be. Maybe you want to take on a new habit. Create a plan and put those things into action!

Sis, this is just the beginning of choosing to do this God's way and not your own way. Even if much work is still ahead, all things are possible through Christ! This is all a part of your healing journey with Christ, the Gentle Healer.

VANESA ALCANTARA

VANESA ALCANTARA

VANESA ALCANTARA

The Unseen War

BECOMING CLEAR ON YOUR MISSION TO HEAL

"GOD'S POWER IS AT WORK TO TEAR DOWN INWARD STRONGHOLDS EVEN WHEN YOUR OUTER CIRCUMSTANCES DON'T LOOK ANY DIFFERENT." -VANESA ALCANTARA

A few months ago, I received a phone call that caught me off guard. Though I didn't recognize the number, I answered, thinking it was a bill collector wanting their money. To my surprise, it was not. The person on the other end of the phone began to inform me that they worked with the FBI and Secret Service, and they had an important message for me. He told me that someone across the country had been using my name and identification and smuggling drugs and thousands of dollars to different states. He knew my name, my address, and other personal information.

I was shocked and had so many questions. My life flashed before my eyes as I began to think about the worst-case scenarios. No one had stolen my identity before. I became so afraid. After forty minutes on the call, I began to suspect that some things were not adding up. Though the information he gave me seemed accurate, I realized from his forceful tone that he was not looking to help me. He suggested that, to get my identity back to its right standing, I needed to "buy it back."

Girl, not only was my heart at the pit of my stomach, but anger began to bubble up like that old boiling water as I realized—this was a scam! This person had devised a plan to convince me I needed to pay him to clean up this identity mess.

As deceptive as this phone call was, Satan's lies are *even more* sophisticated.

The enemy often blindsides and takes advantage of us when we are unaware. He is the ultimate con artist with scams happening in the spiritual realm every day. There are plans to confuse you, deceive you, and ultimately compromise your identity and personhood. But thank God, He reminds us of what is true.

By the end of my phone call, I thought, "You have nothing to be scared of, Vanesa. He is a liar!" And I said as much.

I told the man on the phone, "This doesn't seem right; I'm pretty sure this is a scam." My response set him off! He got really angry and began using more fear tactics to get me to follow his plan. Friend, it's the same thing with the enemy! The enemy of our soul will use fear tactics to get us to fall into his trap and distract us from the Truth. And he gets mad when we call him on it, too! Sometimes we look at our external circumstances and think the battlefield is physically around us, not realizing that the primary battlefield is inward. The enemy knows how easy it is for us to blame people, circumstances, and environments for our challenges. Often, we victimize ourselves and fight the wrong battle, allowing resentment to fill our hearts when we don't progress. Then in moments of pain and desperation, we turn to everything *but* God. We will use personal wisdom, societal norms, and manufactured tactics to overcome our challenges instead of using the God-given weapons and strategies He gives us to win the war.

By the end of the call, I did what we should all do to the enemy himself; I hung up.

Sis, *hang up the phone!*

We've entertained the enemy and his lies for way too long. Wake up and realize that the unseen war is happening, and instead of being sucked into his deceit, I want to help you see how you can gain power and awareness through God's word to finally hang up and do the work to *heal*.

Even when our struggles don't seem particularly spiritual, there is always more to our battles than what meets the eye. Just like this scammer had a hold of my personal information, Satan has been aware of you, your struggles, and your weaknesses all your life. He isn't omnipresent, but he is very, *very* old. He is well-versed in the generational patterns you carry, every childhood wound you've experienced, and every sin propensity for which you are wired. The kingdom of darkness has studied you and your family from the Garden of Eden, and he is an expert on exploiting our wounds and vulnerabilities.

In addition to identifying our diseases, we must uncover how Satan has taken advantage of those unresolved areas and added spiritual oppression wherever possible. He often gains access and even our permission to cling onto us when we fail to live within the safe boundaries of God's way of life. I hate to break it to you, but yes, we open ourselves up to demonic influence and oppression. We often open these doors through unforgiveness, unaddressed sinful behaviors (both ours and in generations before us), and a lack of awareness. The enemy knows exactly how to tempt us, especially when he knows our genetic dispositions.

We must gain a clearer picture of the unseen battle and learn how spiritual warfare works to dismantle the enemy's devices and expose his hidden agendas.

Let's start with the basics...

- **WHO IS GOD?** **(1 Timothy 2:5)**

Our Heavenly Father, Creator, and Source reflected in three persons: God the Father, Jesus Christ the Son, and the Holy Spirit. He is all-powerful, undefeated, and no one is greater.

- **WHO ARE WE?** **(Ephesians 2:10)**

God's beloved children, created for good works, made to know Him, embody Him, represent Him, rule with Him, and enjoy deep fellowship with Him.

- **WHO IS OUR ENEMY?** **(I John 5:19)**

Satan, his kingdom of darkness, the darkened world systems, and our sinful flesh.

- **WHERE IS THE WAR TAKING PLACE?** **(2 Corinthians 10:3–5)**

Primarily in the spirit realm, our minds, and the world systems. Though we see the ripple effects or manifestation in the natural domain, there is always significant activity in the unseen.

What happens in the spirit realm affects the natural realm.

- **WHAT IS THE ENEMY AFTER?** **(John 10:10)**

Satan wants to keep you unaware of his tactics, distort your beliefs, isolate you, disconnect you from God, and influence your behaviors.

- **WHAT WEAPONS AND STRATEGIES DOES THE ENEMY HAVE?** **(2 Corinthians 2:11)**

Ignorance, lies, fear, isolation, sin, generational patterns, false comfort, pride, control, worldly pleasures, and distractions.

- **WHO ARE OUR ALLIES?** **(Luke 22:43)**

The Holy Spirit, the Kingdom of Heaven, angelic help and heavenly reinforcements, the Body of Christ.

- **WHAT WEAPONS AND STRATEGIES DO WE HAVE AVAILABLE? (Ephesians 6:10-20)**

Submission to God, Scripture, knowing and applying the Truth, putting on the armor of God, praise and worship, prayer and fasting, leaning into your God-given community, proclaiming the Name of Jesus, taking hold of the power we receive by the Blood of Jesus.

What a powerful reminder of who and whose we are, and how the battle is taking place!

Perhaps you are thinking, *I'm not sure if this chapter is for me, I'm not really into all this spiritual warfare talk.* Or *What does this have to do with me dealing, healing & growing?*

My Dear Sis, whether you show up to battle or not, you are most definitely a target for the kingdom of darkness and there is no hiding. The enemy has already decided that he is against you and has devised plans to kill, steal, and destroy whatever he can in your life. You might as well rise in the power of God and utilize your heavenly provisions. If the enemy can stop you from dealing, healing and growing, he can stop you from spreading the Truth—the Gospel of Jesus Christ!

Don't allow him to blind you.

There is constant spiritual warfare against you which is mainly unseen. The battle is continuous because the enemy of your soul hates each and every one of God's children. The devil and his pawns are not on team "Inner Healing." And any time you take steps toward Jesus, where you will find healing, wholeness, and Truth, the kingdom of darkness will do everything in its power to deter you.

John 10:9-10 AMP says the following:

> *I am the Door; anyone who enters through Me will be saved [and will live forever], and will go in and out*

[freely], and find pasture (spiritual security). The thief comes only in order to steal and kill and destroy. I came that they may have and enjoy life, and have it in abundance [to the full, till it overflows].

Satan is *hell-bent* on your spiritual destruction. The Bible describes the devil as one who stalks, intimidates, and looks to devour. Scripture says,

Be alert and of sober mind. Your enemy, the devil, prowls around like a roaring lion looking for someone to devour. Resist him, standing firm in the faith, because you know that the family of believers throughout the world is undergoing the same kind of suffering."
1 Peter 5:8-9 NIV

Perhaps you're assessing your life and don't feel particularly attacked by the enemy. But that is part of his deception to *keep you unaware.* One particular breeding ground the enemy loves to attack and sow his destructive seed is in our minds. Our beliefs often go under the radar because we can be stubborn about loosening our grip of thoughts and beliefs that have never served us. The enemy has toyed with our belief systems since the Garden of Eden.

We often forget about our spiritual, inward battle when gearing up to take on life change. We start trying to control our environments and relationships, and we forget the war begins in the spiritual realm. So, the first place of often always the mind. Change does not begin with behavior modification. It starts with our thoughts and beliefs. Transformation starts in the mind. Romans 12:2 NIV says,

Do not conform to the pattern of this world, but be transformed by the renewing of your mind. Then you

will be able to test and approve what God's will is—his good, pleasing, and perfect will.

You can almost tell what someone believes about themselves or others by their behavior. There was a time I literally hid from people in my church lobby. I remember walking in through the back wearing my baseball cap to avoid others because I was going through so much I felt I had nothing to give. Not only that, I felt as though people would be disappointed in me.

My belief at that time was that I was *rejectable*.

It's something I still struggle with. The narrative in my mind said if you show others how broken you feel in the season of your life, everyone will think you are weak and a bother. That thinking led to my self-isolation. Isolation led to negative thoughts, which bred negative mindsets.

Same goes for you, Sis.

When we are in that space, we can easily fall into the trap of making decisions that can be destructive. In our vulnerability, we believe lies instead of God's Truth. Thankfully, God's truth will always remain, and His promises will never change. The reality is we can have a hard time believing His Word at times. But even when we struggle to have faith, God has compassion for us and will help us with our unbelief.

Mark 9:24 (AMP) says,

...I do believe; help [me overcome] my unbelief.

Once we identify how Satan has influenced our beliefs, we must align our thoughts and ideas with Jesus' blueprint. From there, we can (and need to) *immediately* make the necessary adjustments that will help us deal, HEAL and grow. By making this shift in our beliefs, we declare war and proclaim that we submit to the Lord. This gives us the grounds and power to resist the enemy and cause him to scatter like the defeated foe he is.

> *Submit yourselves, then, to God. Resist the devil, and he will flee from you.* James 4:7 NIV (italics mine)

So, if you were to place your soul on a soul scanning machine, what would the state of your soul be today? Is it becoming clear to you that you need to pursue change?

You might find that your soul needs renovation, redemption, and freedom, but you still aren't sure how to go about this change. You are not alone. This next chapter will explore how to move from healing into growing. This will be like a full-blown soul renovation!

Let's pray.

Holy Spirit, please show my sister any wayward way within her that is hindering her healing and growth in You. Gently guide her and firmly remind her that she is loved and cared for by You. Thank you for paying it all on the cross for her. Thank you for the freedom she has in You. Please help her to know You more deeply in this time of rebuilding. In Jesus' Name, amen.

Chapter 7 Challenge: Renewing the Mind

What are some things that have been active in your mind and heart that are not in line with the goal to deal, *heal,* and grow?

_____

_____

_____

_____

_____

_____

_____

_____

_____

_____

_____

_____

_____

_____

_____

_____

_____

_____

VANESA ALCANTARA

Phase III

GROW BEYOND IT...
CHAPTERS 8-10

The first few chapters we were working through brokenness, then to soul renovation, and now we're starting to engage intentional preparation for the future. The next few chapters will focus on how to grow beyond the pain of your past. Now that you know what it means to heal from and deal with the emotional baggage, let's go to the next level. You've gained tools and clarity, so now let's talk about how to go from sitting in your pain to living in your purpose. Let's grow beyond the pain.

Are you still in? Let's do this!

Renovation

REFRESHING THE HOUSE YOUR SOUL IS IN

DO YOU NOT KNOW THAT YOUR BODIES ARE TEMPLES OF THE HOLY SPIRIT, WHO IS IN YOU, WHOM YOU HAVE RECEIVED FROM GOD? YOU ARE NOT YOUR OWN; YOU WERE BOUGHT AT A PRICE. THEREFORE HONOR GOD WITH YOUR BODIES. —1 CORINTHIANS 6:19-20 NIV

As a kid, I remember the excitement my immigrant family members felt when buying their first home. There are not enough words! I have memories of visiting my aunt and uncle's newly purchased home in the early 2000s and at the time, the house felt massive. With their hard-earned money, they invested in something they could call their own in the USA, and I'm sure this felt like a huge accomplishment. Looking back now, I realize they purchased a *fix-er-upper*, but thankfully, they had the vision to see what the house could become. Their house wasn't a mansion by any means. But it *was* a two-story home in the *nice* part of the hood in North Jersey. I remember walking inside after the renovations began. There were no rooms, and the framing of the walls was the only thing left standing. Countless family members, including my parents, would come daily to lend a hand as we all took part in the reconstruction. In very little time, it became clear to me that renovation takes a village. A million decisions later, the old house was renovated and up to code.

When I think of this story, one big thing stands out. There were specific reasons my aunt and uncle chose to purchase that fixer-upper. For starters, they had the finances to take on the purchase. They could see past its flaws because they were confident in their skills and ability to renovate. They knew they could utilize the community around them to accomplish the task. And, before even purchasing, they could see what this house would become.

You and I are also *fixer-uppers* that Jesus has purchased with His blood.

The Messiah looked past our flaws because He was confident in His ability to renovate us. He could work through His community, the Church, to bring out your potential. And long before we were in His possession, He could see what we would become in His hands. This real-life carpenter is a master renovator.

Friend, I assure you that you are in the most capable hands.

Let Him break down every wall that stands in the way of His best for you. Allow His community into your journey and watch how He uses them to help you become stronger and safer. Let him rearrange your home so that His healing and growth will flow out of you. Though it may seem like your inner home may be beyond repair, I want to remind you of the hope you have in Jesus Christ. You may be in a season where you may feel so disconnected from your Christian community and God Himself. But friend, He is closer than you think. Just keep saying, *YES!*

This is the fun part!

In Jesus, you CAN regain a healthy and soulful connection with your Creator through the power of the Holy Spirit. The journey has been challenging, but oh, will it be worth it! Let's look at what a renovation in Christ can look like practically.

Your Soul's Inner Home Inspection

Whenever a certified professional inspects a house, they come prepared with a checklist to assess the home properly and determine if it is safe, sturdy, and up to code. The items on the inspector's list can also be helpful when inspecting *our* inner home.

Allow The Holy Spirit to be your Home Inspector. What might the Holy Spirit report back to you in this moment?

Foundation

Your house must have a firm and level foundation able to hold, stabilize, and sustain you. This will provide the load-bearing strength your house will need to keep it from falling, especially when facing heavy weather conditions that could put your home in danger.

Is your foundation firm?

Structural Damage

It is essential that all exterior and interior walls, ceilings, doors, and windows are leveled and that they don't show any evidence of cracks or damage.

These structures organize and define the spaces within our home. Do you have healthy rhythms and boundaries? Or perhaps, as in the book of Nehemiah, do you have walls that need rebuilding?

Water Damage

Damage from previous floods can result in mold in your home, which can be toxic. Water damage usually comes from storms and excessive rain seeping into your home, especially if you live in a flood zone. The storms of unseen traumas and significant life circumstances can cause damage in our souls, causing permanent erosion. Mold grows where there is darkness. Are you toxic? Have the storms of life caused harm in different areas of your soul? Have you lived in a mental and emotional *zone* that has made you susceptible to damage?

Carbon Monoxide Detectors

The ability to detect harmful gases that may be filling your home is crucial. The placement of these detectors is also critical as they can warn when your air is compromised. Godly friends can be like those kinds of detectors in our life. Are you surrounded by people who quickly alert you when something is *off* in your life?

Sewage System

A proper sewage system in your home is essential for clearing waste properly. We all produce waste that needs to be flushed out of the house constantly. Once that waste is cleared out, it is sent somewhere down a pipe and into a sewer.

As gross as this may sound, we need that same system, not just in our bodies, but in our souls! We need to ensure that there is a proper way of getting rid of our soul waste. We need to rid ourselves of sin and all spiritual toxic waste the world throws our way! So, there must be a proper soul sewage system in place. What does your soul sewer system look like? Are you practicing repentance and eliminating the waste in your soul regularly?

Termites

Termites are those unseen squatters that literally eat up your home from the inside out. These little nasties enter through small openings, cracks, crevices, and crawl space venting. Leaky pipes, improper drainage, and poor airflow create moisture issues that attract termites to come and dwell in your home. Are there spiritual termite oppressors at work within you? Have *leaky areas* or *improper drainage* opened the door for the enemy to come in and create an infestation of lies?

Wiring

If our wiring is damaged, it can cause a fire. How many fires have we had to put out because our mindsets, un-surrendered personalities, and lifestyle habits were not reflecting God's Word? When you have the correct wiring, your electricity works, gives you effective and safe light. Is your wiring system faulty? Do not be fooled by the enlightenment practices of this age. The entangled, twisted worldviews that culture popularizes can wrap and trap you. Some mindsets and lifestyles seem well-lit, but if you look closer, those flickering lights are a fire waiting to happen.

HVAC

To ensure that the atmosphere of your inner home is safe and refreshing, we must have proper ventilation, and our air filters must be clean. Can the Holy Spirit move freely to heat, ventilate, and cool your inner home as needed? Are there any blockages not allowing the Holy Spirit to flow in you?

As you allow the Holy Spirit to do a home inspection, you may find that several areas need attention.

Many of these areas we've already addressed in the dealing and healing phases but now it's time to rebuild and learn how refreshing our souls will activate growth!

Renovation & Refurnishing

Congratulations, it is time to renovate! Thankfully you've already put in some work in this area!

Looking at what needs to be done and doing it are two different things. You've gone to town demolishing the works of the enemy found in your soul. You've exposed lies and sinful patterns that have been holding you back. You've torn down rotted walls and old structures from your inner home. And now, you are left with a home ready for refurnishing. These next steps will fill your home with Truth and life. It's time to refurnish, allowing God to do what only He can do! Making room for Him to fill us as He sees fit is the best remodel we can ever ask for.

God is not only the ultimate restorer but also *the master architect* and *the expert interior designer*. Not only that, He KNOWS YOU! As you sit with the architect of your soul, you will find that his designs are absolutely masterful. Jeremiah 29:11 NIV says,

> *"For I know the plans I have for you,'" declares the Lord, "plans to prosper you and not to harm you, plans to give you hope and a future."'*

The more he shows you what He has in store, the more your wants and inclinations will shift. He will place NEW desires in you. He will renew your perspective and help you see that His vision for you is much higher than what you could develop for yourself. And when He has completed His work, His heavenly signature will be undeniably evident in you. God created us to represent Him on earth, displaying His love, character, and glory from the inside out.

Can you trust Him to use the good, the bad, and the ugly to form you, refine you, and use you to display His glory?

God has fashioned us with purpose in mind. He has prepared works for us to do that He has equipped us for. There may even be untapped rooms and unseen areas in you that God has prepared you to access at an ordained time to accomplish the work He has called you to do. So, what are those good works? What has God created you to do? A good starting place may be the purposes for which we were ALL created. We were created to:

- Have intimacy with God (John 17:3)

- Pursue holiness (Ephesians 1:4)

- Walk in humility (Micah 6:8)

- Do good works (Ephesians 2:10)

- Exhibit the Fruit of the Spirit (Galatians 5:22-23)

- Show Gospel hospitality, loving and serving those who seem difficult to love (1Peter 4:8-9)

- Live on mission, making disciples (Matthew 28:19-20)

- Display His glory (Isaiah 43:7)

- Have dominion (Genesis 1:26)

- Love the Lord God and our neighbor (Mark 12:30-31)

Renewing our minds with these truths will renovate our entire inner home. What do you think it would look like to consult God, the Architect and Designer of your inner home? There are things He has already defined as part of His design for you just like the ones mentioned above. Ask Him to reveal His blueprint and how He wants to fill your inner home.

Friend, you are not alone. I need these reminders too! Often, themes of rejection, loss of identity, loneliness, and a constant fear of abandonment still come up for me. Though God has done so much healing in me throughout the years I still have a long way to go! I praise God that His Grace is enough. His love covers us, He forgives our sins and heals our pain. Regardless of how many times we trip and fall into old destructive patterns and beliefs, we can STILL run to our Heavenly Father.

I have poured countless hours of prayer throughout the years, with many journals to prove it, spending sometimes tearful and heart wrenching moments with Jesus. No matter how difficult things get, we cannot allow our challenges or mess-ups to keep us from who and what we were created for. Just like you, I have seasons when prayer and journaling are not going so well and maybe even feel like a chore at times. But it doesn't take long to realize that the only one who can bring me out of whatever mud I'm stuck in, is Jesus, our Redeemer, our Savior. Friend, I've seen Him come through too many times to doubt Him now. I can say with full certainty that that God doesn't waste a thing. What the enemy means for evil, God turns it around for our good and for His glory.

Sis, it's time to organize yourself with new foundations. It's time to have a deep, powerful, soul renovation with Jesus. When we go through the process of a soul renovation and toss all our soul's rubble into the "dumpster," we make room for God to fill our souls with His presence. This soul work is worth it, my Friend!

Let us pray:

Heavenly Father, I pray for my sister in Christ. Thank you for the wondrous work You have started in and through her. The remodel-ing can be painful, but you have a greater purpose in mind. I pray that you will help her discover your plans, purpose, and intentions for her life. Please help her to see what you see and want what you want. Help my sister stand firm in the JOY you have set before her. Give her the resilience to endure her cross daily and clothe herself with Christ. Remind her that whom the Son has set free is free indeed! She IS free by YOUR power and might. In the mighty Name of Jesus, I pray, Amen.

Chapter 8 Challenge: New Foundations

Reflect and journal on what you've learned in this chapter. What is the Lord speaking to you? Pray and invite the Holy Spirit to fill every space once occupied by the enemy. Write down what you want Him to refurnish within you.

You may even want to consider taking some time to fast and reread this chapter.

For encouragement, see Who I Am in Christ in the Resources section of this book. Discover all amazing things to say about you and let God's truth shape your identity as you dive deeper into His Word.

_____

_____

_____

_____

_____

_____

_____

_____

_____

_____

_____

_____

_____

_____

_____

_____

_____

_____

_____

VANESA ALCANTARA

VANESA ALCANTARA

Soul Growth

"YOU ARE WHAT YOU EAT." AND SO IT WILL BE WITH YOUR SOUL.

THE RIGHTEOUS WILL FLOURISH LIKE A PALM TREE, THEY WILL GROW LIKE A CEDAR OF LEBANON; PLANTED IN THE HOUSE OF THE LORD, THEY WILL FLOURISH IN THE COURTS OF OUR GOD. THEY WILL STILL BEAR FRUIT IN OLD AGE, THEY WILL STAY FRESH AND GREEN. —PSALMS 92:12-14 NIV

Make the Word of God your favorite meal! The word of God is alive and powerful. It's our bread of life and nourishment to our souls. I was always one of those people who swore I could never take on a healthy eating lifestyle. It felt impossible and too expensive. I remember my husband and I looking at our budget and realized, in a single month, we had spent hundreds of dollars on fast food! We decided right then that we had to make a significant change. Sure, the healthier the food was, the higher the price tended to be.

But as we continued to change, the satisfaction we received from nourishing our bodies also reduced the need to eat constantly.

We began to experience greater satisfaction because we consumed better quality foods. The investment in our healthy eating paid off well. Friend, It's the same at a soul level, AND YOU ARE WORTH IT.

Feeding your soul the good stuff is costly but worth it. It will cost you time and energy, but the results will be incredible! This way of feeding your soul produces life and I am confident you will be able to do this through the power of the Holy Spirit!

I have found that the start of a good meal is knowing what its made of and having a plan on how to make it. To make good nutritious meals for your soul, you must realize that all you have is all you need. Allow me to be your *soul nutritionist* for the moment. Let us look at a few "Good Meals," using what you already have in your pantry. It seems strange, but this is what will start the journey to take your soul work to the next level. These are essential:

PB&J

In our day to day a PB&J may not be considered a completely healthy snack. But on a spiritual level, this is really good eatin'!! And, for the record, we all need a good spiritual PB&J for the remainder of our lives.

- **Prayer**

- **B**ible Studying/Journaling/Reflecting

- **J**ourneying with others

In the natural, this is a comfort food or a quick meal, but spiritually these are superfoods! It may surprise you that the simplest of ingredients may make the most delicious foods. Bread, jelly, and peanut butter go a long way! Let's break these down and see how they apply to the soul foods available to you!

PRAYER

We've already touched on this topic earlier in the book, but there is something specific I need you to know. Your constant communication with God will be crucial in this next phase of your healing journey. Prayer is the umbilical cord that keeps continual conversation with God flowing back and forth transferring nutrients to your soul.

Charles Spurgeon said, "a neglected prayer closet is the beginning of all spiritual decline."

Prayer keeps you connected to your Source, in line with His will and focused on the main thing, which is *Him*. Talking with God will help you find direction in life. The Holy Spirit will lead you—through prayer—to make the right decisions. And it will empower you to resist the enemy in times of trouble.

In my walk with God, I've received strategies and instruction for my life through prayer. This whole book is a result of prayer!

Prayer can be the same for you.

As a child, I remember hearing people talk about "prayer closets." I found out that Matthew 6:6 tells us to "close the door behind you and pray in secret." I took that seriously and converted my small, narrow, closet into my personal prayer closet. I kept my bible and a journal in there and would go to spend time with God. I was about 11 years old at the time. At such a young age, I believe the Holy Spirit was showing me something important. Time with God is enjoyable, it's an adventure, it's a space where He and I can have intimate conversations, if I let it.

I carried this prayer space inside of me throughout the years. As I evolved through the different stages of life, pre-teen, teens, young adult years, I've never stopped praying. Through ups and downs, sinful slip-ups and all, I still kept the communication going even if it was a simple, "Jesus, I need you."

Regardless of what life looks like for you today, you can have the prayer life that you've always wanted. Keep pressing forward, and don't give up talking to God because it doesn't look like what you want it to be. Letting go of prayer strategies and methods that worked in a previous season is hard. Trust me, I still struggle with this today! But learning to lean in and pray without ceasing is essential. You must adapt to different ways of constant prayer *in every season*.

1 Thessalonians 5:16-18 NIV says,

> *Rejoice always, pray continually, give thanks in all circumstances; for this is God's will for you in Christ Jesus.*

The breakdown of this verse is interesting. These are instructions for that inner intimate space. I see this as food. You should think of seeing it that way, too. To rejoice is to show great joy and delight. This is extremely difficult to do when you are going through dark seasons. But somehow the Holy Spirit gives us this capability through the *strength* in our prayer muscles. Giving thanks in all circumstances is a byproduct of that muscle, as is the endurance needed to pray continually.

Friends, this does not depend solely on us.

We are not so powerful that we can conjure up the strength to make this amazing prayer life happen on our own. It doesn't show up because of all the hard work *we've* put into it! That is pride rearing its ugly head. We need the Holy Spirit. Through Him we can do all things.

There have been seasons where I've felt like my prayer life was stale. I sat down in the silence waiting for words to magically appear only to allow anxiety to rise up as I begin thinking of the laundry, dishes, play dates, friend dates, and all the other things I had to do! I would feel terrible about not knowing what to say.

I've later learned that there are resources to help us in this area! I've included them in this book for you.

In the Resource section of this book, you will find prayer models that can help guide you. I have personally used some of these and they have all been a great help in spicing up my prayer life. Scripture says,

> *My people are destroyed for lack of knowledge.*
> Hosea 4:6 NIV

Don't let your prayer life perish because of lack of knowledge. Look through your options today. Hit the refresh button on your prayer life because God is happily waiting for you to come back into that prayer closet.

BIBLE STUDY

A great follow-up to good chats with God is good meals with Him. Making a practice of being in God's Word every day is crucial to your spiritual development. To continue to grow beyond your past, you must invest time in feasting from His word. We spend so much time consuming everything around us and it so easily draws us away from Him. We live in a culture where there is very little protection from information overload. From social media to the news, pop culture drama, family text threads, and all the other latest pieces of information...it's all too much! These things beg for our attention, and we give in to them and feed off the feelings they serve us. Fear, anger, hopelessness, despair...they are all waiting for you, one text away.

But when you make it a habit to fill yourself with His word, above all else and before anything else, things begin to shift in your life. Priorities start to get aligned with God's Truth and we begin to pour out what we've let in.

Some wise words in Proverbs 4:23 NIV tell us,

> *Above all else, guard your heart, for everything you do flows from it.*

This verse cautions us to guard our hearts above all else, because it's an entry point into our mind, body and soul. Once something is in your heart (whatever it is), the actions will follow. Whatever has been flowing out of you in your words and actions has been a result of what you've allowed into your heart. If your heart functioned as a mouth (as an entry point into your body), what have you been feeding it lately?

I've known many people who love reading the Bible in a year or take on various challenges to try and meet different Bible reading goals. Regardless of how you do it, *getting the Word in you* is the point. Coming up with a Bible study plan is the same as meal planning. When you know ahead of time what you will consume later on in the week, it can help put you at ease. When we open up the Bible, we often feel lost, confused, or bored by what's in there! Thankfully, some resources can help you with Bible-reading strategies and methods to keep you engaged and fed.

For more information on these resources check out the resource section. But for now, let's talk about the next part in the superfood spiritual meal!

JOURNEYING WITH OTHERS

The people you surround yourself with in this process are essential to your healing. Jesus, Himself had 12 disciples, and of them, three were closest to Him. We all need to surround ourselves with God-fearing people who can pray, give wise counsel, and sharpen us. Within a healthy community, you can (hopefully) find 1-2 people you trust. Have them hold you accountable for the things you are trying to heal or improve. When you feel weak and know you are spiraling, text them, call them, go see them. Don't keep people out of your situation. Invite them to your process.

Now, I'm aware that sometimes due to a lack of trust, we hold people at arm's length for fear of getting hurt again. When we push others out, there are good things we keep from ourselves, too. We push away support, love, and a cheerleading squad that will keep you going when you want to give up! If you need to find a new group of friends, do so. Put yourself out there! Show yourself to be friendly (Proverbs 18:24 NIV), like it says in the Bible! Get plugged into your local church. Maybe even find faith-based online communities. Pray and ask the Holy Spirit for guidance in this. He will lead you to the community He has for you.

Communicating feelings and needs can be very difficult for some people. It can take time to find out what is going on internally. Nevertheless, give yourself the space and permission to feel and communicate these feelings. If you find it difficult to pinpoint your feelings, check out the Feeling Wheel in the resources section. It is helpful to see several emotions laid out to identify the ones that resonate most for you. I would encourage you, my sweet friend, to share these thoughts and feelings with God and a trusted friend.

If I can be real with you, everyone can use a therapist!

Communicating with a professional counselor can be life changing. Those kinds of professionals can offer tools and strategies that can be super beneficial to your process. In addition, the Holy Spirit can work through a counselor to help you heal areas in your life where others cannot help you because they don't have professional training. Finding a therapist that fits the criteria or has the chemistry you desire may be challenging. Still, it's worth the risk of trying one. And thankfully, there are no strings attached! If it didn't work out with one, then try another! The longer you avoid it, the longer you will carry unnecessary weight. Just give it a shot and stop listening to the voices that tell you it won't work and that it's too hard. Ask the Lord to help you overcome your hesitation. You won't know until you try it.

You are not where you started. Your job now is to plant seeds into your soul that will reap a harvest that will feed and nurture your children's children (biological, non-biological, mentees, friends, and family). Make the choice to journey with those who want you to grow. And for the record, whether or not you try, you have people journeying with you. They are an integral part of your journey with the Lord.

Watch Your Cravings

Have you ever had cravings you couldn't resist? The kind of intense desire for something that you would lose your mind if you didn't get it?

While pregnant with my firstborn, I experienced cravings in ways I will never forget! I loved chicken patties—they were my weakness. As part of my routine appointments, I would see a nutritionist, and we constantly discussed my eating habits. I remember sitting at the edge of my seat, ready to leave before the appointment even began! The nutritionist would make her grand entrance and sit with me to review all the food and drink items I needed to remove from my diet. Yet again, she would tell me that I needed to stop gaining weight and gain more self-control.

"We are a bit concerned with the weight you are putting on; you could be borderline diabetic, and the baby is already measuring big for her stage."

But I kept eating those patties.

As a result of not following the doctor's orders, my eating habits complicated things inside my body so much that it affected my labor and delivery. It was just as the doctor predicted. I learned that my choices had the potential to shift the outcome for better or for worse. My food choices grew my syrup baby to a whopping 9 lbs and 21 inches long baby girl, who ultimately ended up a c-section.

All because of food choices.

Friend, now that we've dealt with the things that have cluttered our souls, causing us to crave things that are not beneficial, I want us to focus on the soul foods that will bring refreshment, life, and vibrancy to your soul, to your "home." I'm talking about more spiritual PB&J! What can you be feeding your soul that will help you become strong and build endurance and stamina in your walk with Christ? What good things can you feed your mind, will, and emotions?

Stay Motivated

Sometimes we can underutilize the provisions God builds into our everyday lives. You would be surprised at the impact of simply getting proper rest, eating good meals, breathing fresh air, and getting some vitamin D from the sun. Let's be honest, our lives can get pretty busy. Our schedules are full of all kinds of responsibilities. We can find ourselves tired, overwhelmed, and just trying to survive. The *last* thing we want to do in those moments is add what feels like the massive task of caring for our souls.

But if we don't, we will only worsen our inner state and make life that much harder for ourselves. So, we have to prioritize this holy, soulful work, and do everything we can to stay motivated!

Oftentimes, the distresses of our lives and the constant reminders of what is not working feel like they work against you and deplete your desire to do the work. However, those are the moments that we have to push past our discomfort and our discouragement and strengthen ourselves in the Lord.

> *And David was greatly distressed, for the people spoke of stoning him, because all the people were bitter in soul, each for his sons and daughters. But David strengthened himself in the Lord his God.* 1 Samuel 30:6 ESV

When it's a sunny day out and the birds are chipping, it puts me in a great mood! Elevating your mood can be extremely helpful in assessing motivation. When I feel down and overwhelmed, I often

127

go on a short walk, listen to fun music, and enjoy the pause in my day. Then I'll listen to a sermon or podcast about the theme that is overwhelming me, and I feel that hope begins to grow in my heart. Vision for what is possible floods my mind, and it motivates me. It's amazing how even a few minutes of refreshment can bring our moods up and help us gain some motivation. Even when going outside is not an option, you can make your favorite beverage and sit with a good book or journal, or spend a few minutes learning or doing a hobby.

Remember the soul buckets from before? Filling your tank is so important. When we elevate our mood, it emotionally levels us so that we move toward motivation. If nature itself praises the Lord, you can definitely use that for filling up when you are feeling a little low.

As women, we can pour out so much and may even feel defined by the ways we pour out. But we are not indestructible. We need to recharge. And as selfish or irresponsible as you may feel for taking time to recharge or investing in your sense of motivation, it is the greatest gift you can give to the people you serve.

Yes! You are a gift, especially when you are a full and motivated you!

What motivates you, my friend? Search it out. When you are in a slump, what pulls you back up? When you are feeling good, what keeps your mood going? When nothing seems to be working, where does your mind go? These are great questions to ask yourself to create a plan for when you need a pick-me-up.

Lean into encouraging your soul. Give yourself a chance to try something new in this season. In the Psalms, David would tell his soul to praise the Lord in his darkest moments. It shows us that we won't always feel like doing the right thing or sticking to a healthy frame of thought. Our feelings are horrible masters. But our feelings are fleeting!

I want you to speak to your soul and remind it of God's faithfulness and goodness. When you feel weak and discouraged, put on your favorite worship music! Research sermons regarding what you are struggling with—disappointment, motherhood, friendships, lust, fear, worry, anxiety, depression, etc., and watch or listen to them! Keeping your eyes fixated on things that will bring light and life is critical!

Matthew 6:22 AMP speaks of the eyes being the window to our souls, and it says:

> *The eye is the lamp of the body; so if your eye is clear [spiritually perceptive], your whole body will be full of light [benefiting from God's precepts]. But if your eye is bad [spiritually blind], your whole body will be full of darkness [devoid of God's precepts]. So if the [very] light inside you [your inner self, your heart, your conscience] is darkness, how great and terrible is that darkness!*

Whatever we let through our eyes will be reflected in our thoughts, emotions, and actions. Whether light or dark, it will affect your motivation or lack thereof. It's just like eating junk food. If we allow the light of Christ to shine into our eye-gates and submerge ourselves in His truth, we will reflect Him in times of dire need. May His Truths be so hidden in the walls of your heart and soul that, in the hard seasons, YOU CAN REMIND YOURSELF of the Truth you already know.

Speak to your soul:

I am more than a conqueror!
When I am weak, then I'm strong!
I am not alone!
He sees me.

Why, my soul, are you downcast? Why so disturbed within me? Put your hope in God, for I will yet praise him, my Savior and my God. Psalm 42:11 NIV

Chapter 9 Challenge: Soul Snacks

I challenge you to share your story on these pages, and then, consider sharing these pages with someone else. Start your journey with someone you know. Sow seeds of hope, love, and faith in the lives of others so they can see that they, too, can experience transformation in Christ.

_____
_____
_____
_____
_____
_____
_____
_____
_____
_____
_____
_____
_____
_____
_____
_____
_____
_____
_____
_____
_____
_____

VANESA ALCANTARA

10

The Garden Enclosed

THE LORD WILL SURELY COMFORT ZION AND WILL LOOK WITH COMPAS-SION ON ALL HER RUINS; HE WILL MAKE HER DESERTS LIKE EDEN, HER WASTELANDS LIKE THE GARDEN OF THE LORD. JOY AND GLADNESS WILL BE FOUND IN HER, THANKSGIVING AND THE SOUND OF SINGING.
—Isaiah 51:3 NIV

How you live your life sets the tone for the next generation.

Sounds daunting, doesn't it? You are sowing seeds that will produce life or death—not just for you but for your children and anyone else you influence. The older I get, the more I appreciate the seeds my family planted in my heart when I was a little girl. For example, living a life of prayer and devotion to God was a seed my family planted in me.

Growing up, my parents would talk about the greatness of God. They would be transparent about our needs, our lack, and what they prayed and believed God would do. And I saw God's hand in our lives often in numerous circumstances. The power of prayer and trust in the move of the Holy Spirit was planted and watered inside me for years.

There is a fundamental principle here. Anything you plant and nurture will grow. And you will be known by your fruit.

Earlier in the book, we worked through a house analogy and described the work God wants to do in our inner home. Now, I want us to walk through the back door and spend some time in the soil of our backyard. We touched on the garden, but now we're really getting into the things that will have a long-term effect.

Imagine your soul's backyard as a place where you plant seeds, grow vegetation, and feed the people around you. If you know people with backyards, you know it is an easy part of the home to leave unattended. Maybe it's just our house, but our backyard looks like there is a yard sale in the jungle most days. The toys and outdoor equipment are enveloped by the tall overgrown grass all around it. That neglect has a cost, and that cost can stop your yard from being fruitful and abundant.

Tending to Your New Growth

So ask yourself: What qualities, attributes, and values do you want to see grow? It's that simple.

If there are things you DO NOT want to grow in your spirit/soul/body, but they are currently in your greenhouse, you can uproot them today.

Yes! Right now.

Let's walk through your inner greenhouse together.

Look at the different categories below (this is like cleaning the house, but now we are tending to your garden). What habits and sin patterns have you identified that you need to uproot? Whether these belong to your family or come from within yourself, let's uproot all the things that don't belong.

These all began with a choice, a thought that led to a belief that created a whole mindset around a lie that has hindered God's purposes for your life! God designed you to produce and grow greatness, but hanging onto these weeds will not get you there! So, let's elevate our thinking and rise to the challenge. When the world tells you to do what makes you happy and live your truth, how do you stand your ground and pursue holiness? How will you live differently from the world?[1]

Are you willing to be an example of true freedom and strength? Let's sow some new thoughts, ideas, and truths about who you are and who God has called you to be!

You can do this, friend.

I loved these statements I read from Pastor Craig Groeschel from Life Church in Edmond, Oklahoma. I've paraphrased a few of these and added in Scripture references. The following spiritual truths are anchors for our identity in Christ. They can free you from strongholds and create new life inside your heart, mind, and soul!

Read these out loud if you can!

- I am the daughter of the King of kings (Revelation 17:14).

- God has given me everything I need to do what He's called me to do (2 Peter 1:3).

- I will speak encouraging, life-giving words and build others up (Hebrews 10:24-25).

- The joy of the Lord is my strength (Nehemiah 8:10).

- I will not compare myself to other women (Galatians 6:4-5).

- I will uphold God's standards and measure myself with grace (Romans 12:3).

- I will love and laugh rather than fight and complain (Philippians 2:14-16).

---

1. Romans 12:2 NIV

- I refuse to waste my life on meaningless things (Ecclesiastes 3:18-22).

- I will act justly, love mercy, a n d walk humbly with my God (Micah 6:8).

- Through Christ, I am strong and able (Philippians 4:13).

- Through Christ, I am gentle, compassionate and able to forgive (Colossians 3:12-13).

- I will fight the good fight for what matters most (2 Timothy 4:7).

- Because of Jesus, I lack nothing (Psalm 34:10).

I want you to carve out some time today. Get yourself a comfy place, maybe play some instrumental worship music. Ask the Holy Spirit to sit in this with you. Invite Him into each section of your inner greenhouse. And pray the following prayer before you move to the next sections:

Heavenly Father, I come humbly before You. You know I am a sinner. There are sin patterns here that I can't uproot myself. Forgive me of my sins and uproot all these things (fill in the blank if you wish). None of these glorify You or serve me. Take each of these things and wipe me clean. Down from the root, yank these out in Jesus' Name and toss them to the ocean's depths like Your word says in Micah 7:19.

Forgive me for how I have nurtured and watered lies, sinful thoughts, and destructive habits. I admit that I have created idols and produced destruction by tending to them. Forgive me.

I turn my heart towards You today. I love You. Fill my greenhouse with Your presence. Let Your love flood my whole being. Give me the mind of Christ. I ask You to invade every part of me.

Father, help me be an example to my family and those around me of what it means to die to the self and live for You. Help me to live a truly abundant life in the mighty Name of Jesus. AMEN!

Sweet Seeds

I come from a big Dominican family. Growing up, we often met at my grandmothers' house, especially on Fridays. Still, even if we showed up on a random Wednesday, one thing we knew for sure was that there would be food. And not just enough for a serving of four. It was more like a serving of 20.

That is not an exaggeration.

My grandmother taught all her 13 children, especially the ten women, how to cook, starting at the age of nine. I wish I could tell you there were recipes for our delicious cultural dishes, but there are not. We all learned by observing and trying. Not only did my aunts, uncles, and parents make a meal for all the members of their immediate family in a house, but they also had to make enough for extended family AND surrounding neighbors who may swing by unannounced!

It was the tradition then and still is now.

As I've mentioned, I do not come from a wealthy family. When my mom was growing up in the Dominican Republic, she experienced extreme poverty. My grandmother usually cooked their meals outside in fire pits using pots and charcoal. The scarcity was intense. My mom and her siblings have memories of seeing their mother leaning against the back doorway of their home, looking straight ahead at her backyard. They would see her eyes well up in tears as she wondered how she would feed her children that day.

I can only imagine the weight she must have felt—the burden and responsibility to provide. But also, Dominican culture is very hospitable, so she bore shame and sadness also. If anyone passed by, she would have nothing to offer them. I can see her in my mind with her hair wrapped up in the heat of the day and a dust-filled apron wrapped around her waist. I imagine her waiting for God to show up for her, and not only because of her kids' empty stomachs. She was also believing for provision for the other people she knew would come to enjoy her food. My grandmother portioned the food for her children so they had enough to bless others if they ever needed food.

She sowed seeds of generosity, not realizing how God would later bless her life and the lives of her children and her children's children. They went from living in poverty to coming to the United States, where they all looked forward to a fresh start. All of her children worked hard and trusted God every step of the way, doing their best with what they had and what they knew. They grew their lives from the little my grandmother had buried in the ground and still do now, decades later. I am a product of those planted seeds, flourishing in the land she could have never dreamt up for herself.

You may have a story like that as well.

Maybe your grandfather sacrificed his life in such a way that made way for you and your family to be where you are today. Perhaps the values they planted within your family are values and morals you still hold. Maybe it was your mother's drive to raise you and your siblings (if you have them) differently, so she made sacrifices to be there for you in ways her mother wasn't there for her. Or maybe a non-biological parent came into your life and loved you so powerfully that it uprooted lies you didn't even know you believed about yourself. These could be in your soil, and you may have little information. You may know your parents and guardians, but much more comes to light when you know about their soil.

Their soil holds their stories, memories, traumas, and triumphs. The seed they planted (that you may or may not be eating) is the product of a situation. That situation led them to a feeling, which led them to a belief. Their belief led them to a decision, and that decision led them to sow seeds (with words or bold moves). You are eating the fruit that they planted, whether it is flourishing or languishing. But here and now, you have a chance to fill your soul with seeds that can be nurtured differently because you've done the work. *Healed you* is a much better gardener than *wounded you*. When we live a life surrendered to the Holy Spirit, He can guide our hands to work the ground he so graciously has given to us. With that in mind, here are some SOUL SEEDS you can fill your refreshed soil with and water daily with the Word of God:

- FORGIVENESS: When you sow seeds of forgiveness, you will enjoy the fruit of true freedom.

- PEACE: If you water peace, you will see it circulate and purify the air in your home.

- JOY: Declare that joy will flow out from you and unto your family like a river.

- PATIENCE: Is a virtue cultivated in the soil of surrender.

- TRUTH: Speak a language of life with the accent of wisdom & kindness.

- IDENTITY: Christ in me is all I need.

- WEALTH: In knowledge, wisdom, love, generosity, finances and God-honoring discipline.

- HEALTH: Mental, emotional, physical & spiritual.

- CREATIVITY: Allow God's purpose for you to color everything you do.

- HEALING: Healthy progression in a forward motion to always lead a healed life.

- FREEDOM: In Christ, we find our freedom.

- WARRIOR: Water the fighter in you through prayer & declaration of scriptures.

- SERVING: Your spouse, your family, your community, and your friends.

- SELF-CARE: Caring for your mind, body, and soul is essential.

- REST: If God rested on the 7th day, you need rest, too.

- BEAUTY: You are God's masterpiece. You have beauty inside and out.

- GENEROSITY: It's better to give than to receive.

Toxic Weeds

The way we manage our Soul Seeds can be either life-giving or life-choking. We must be vigilant about what is inside our soil as well as any stubborn little weeds that are trying to stick around. Truthfully, some seeds in our soil never carried a sweet sentiment. Some seeds got mixed up and placed in us by the negative words spoken over us. Maybe a person close to you scared you by planting an idea in your mind that you will never amount to anything. Perhaps you've been told that you are "just like your mother or father," pointing to a negative quality they've carried and now, someone has declared that over you. Maybe promiscuity was sown in your soil via sexual abuse. Someone came in and violated your greenhouse and took advantage of your innocence because of their own broken pain and past.

Maybe religiosity was planted into your soil, meant to give you life, but it began to feel suffocating and confusing. Your family went to church several days out of the week and instilled toxic beliefs and twisted truths about God's love in you. They preached condemnation without compassion or grace. Throughout time, weeds of shame, guilt, and pressures to please everyone squeezed the life out of you, causing you to bow out and hold hatred against the church.

These my friends are toxic weeds that can choke out the good seeds if we aren't careful and thorough. It breaks my heart to think of the many women lost in their pain, seeking other ways to self-medicate and explore alternative *spiritual* options. The personal perception and experiences of God that their family impressed upon them caused so much pain. Instead of seeds flourishing, hurt spoils their soil, leaving them overflowing with weeds of anger and doubt. Misrepresentations of God eclipse the truth of the God they once loved and sought in their time of need. Suddenly, God becomes a cruel puppet master out to get them when the truth is anything but that! He is full of unconditional love and passion for us. Unless awareness arises within the hearts of women in this state of being, they will continue to live empty lives void of a genuine relationship with God.

If only we could see how readily available God is to us! We have a forgiving, tender, strong, loving, and powerful Heavenly Father. Still, instead, the thought processes of the world have consumed their souls to the point that they consider their Christian faith unnecessary. "You are the hero of your own story. Live to please yourself and do what makes you happy."

These empty, non-commitment beliefs to temporary pleasure lead some to success and money. Still, essentially, the route leads to death. The lack of knowledge of the Creator of the universe will cause us a million little deaths inside of us.

My people are being destroyed because they don't know me. Since you priests refuse to know me, I refuse to recognize you as my priests. Since you have forgotten the laws of your God, I will forget to bless your children. Hosea 4:6 NIV

Other versions say, *my people perish for lack of knowledge.*

Consider this. Is it possible that weeds of death and lack of knowledge have compromised sections of your greenhouse? There may be things in your history that you may think are irrelevant and useless information for your life today, but they aren't. My Sister-Friend, I hope that, by now, you can see the importance of your history and how it's affecting your story.

It doesn't have to end here, Sis.

I encourage you to go to these deep places in your soul and invite the Holy Spirit to help you heal and deal so that you can grow beyond the mess! Though this part can be quite uncomfortable, stay with me, it will be worth every minute!

Even by continuing to read, you are doing something powerful. Not many people choose this part of their healing journey. I encourage you to take a stand in the Spirit and clean up your greenhouse! I'm sure you probably have many emotions, memories, or even questions coming up. But know that Christ is for you and is bringing your greenhouse back to life!

The LORD will surely comfort Zion and will look with compassion on all her ruins; he will make her deserts like Eden, her wastelands like the garden of the LORD. Joy and gladness will be found in her, thanksgiving and the sound of singing. Isaiah 51:3 NIV

That is beautifully said.

God will take your ruins and make them into a stunning garden filled with life again! You will find joy and gladness. Your gratitude will form a song you've never sung before. A majestic symphony will emerge from your life, blessing all who interact with you, all because of His touch and your yes.

Chapter 10 Challenge: Committed to Growth

Write down a few seeds you are committed to watering and some weeds are determined to uproot.

VANESA ALCANTARA

VANESA ALCANTARA

Post Soul Scan Care

Now What?

"YOU NEED A CLEAR PLAN FOR YOUR SOUL TO KEEP THINGS CLEAN AND HEALTHY IN YOUR HEART, MIND, AND SOUL." —VANESA ALCANTARA

Jesus went through the *Transportation Security Administration* of life, and they found nothing on Him. And though He did not sin, He watched us go through the *TSA* of our life, watched as we set off the machines and He jumped in. He claimed all our toxicity and sinful patterns as His own.

Friend, you've done so much hard work! You should celebrate getting this far!

I hope you feel very accomplished. I am so proud of you, but most of all, your Heavenly Father is pleased and proud. As you continue your work, you must have a plan for going forward. You don't want to put this book down and trust that everything will come to mind when it should. This is not the end of it. This is only the beginning.

You need a maintenance plan to keep things clean and healthy in your heart, mind, body and soul. For example, suppose you cleaned your house once a year and lived in it without picking it up, throwing trash out, or cleaning it. Things would quickly turn into an episode of Hoarders (in the spiritual realm)! The television show "Hoarders" documents the lives of people who continuously accumulate loads and loads of items, trinkets, trash, old memories, etc. Those homeowners need enormous help getting out of the mess and the mindset that keeps them bound to their hoarding addiction. These people end up having interventions from other family members because the concern for them is so great.

Now maybe that was you at the beginning of this book! And praise God! Because girl, you made it *so far*! I hope these words have served as an intervention for your soul!

I pray you feel more prepared and empowered to pursue your God-given purpose. The tools you've gained here have hopefully blessed you and were eye-opening to what you have inside you and what your true identity can accomplish. Awaken to God's truth and the weapons available within the Scriptures to overcome and scan your soul as you go through life. As you continue allowing the Word of God to scan your soul, He will help you get rid of all the things inside your baggage that have caused you delays, setbacks, and extra weight throughout your life.

I love Hebrews 12:1-3 in The Message version. I've added my reactions to it because why not! Read it slowly and read it out loud to your soul. Just like David would talk to his soul in the Psalms. Say it out loud wherever you are. If you are in a public place and don't want to shout like you got no sense, whisper it to yourself.

Do you see what this means—all these pioneers who blazed the way (Your family, friends, mentors, leaders—your community that is here on earth and in heaven), all these veterans cheering us on? It means we'd better get on with it (Get yourself ready!!). Strip down (like in the TSA, take off and out any extra weight that doesn't belong), start running—and never quit! No extra spiritual fat, no parasitic sins. Keep your eyes on Jesus, who both began and finished this race we're in. Focus on Him! Study how He did it, using tools and strategies in the Scriptures. Study how He did it (tools and strategies in the scriptures). Because He never lost sight of where He was headed—that exhilarating finish in and with God—He could put up with anything along the way: The cross, shame, whatever. And now He's there on the other side of the battle, in the place of honor, right alongside God. When you find yourselves flagging in your faith, go over that story again, item by item, that long litany of hostility He plowed through. That will shoot adrenaline into your souls!

Jesus is our ultimate example of how to live life on this side of Heaven. The way he ran His race and kept His eyes on the Father, knowing that it would cost Him His LIFE—that is a real role to model. Jesus was persecuted, talked about, beaten with words, and beaten by human hands. He endured lies and humiliation, taking it all on with you in mind. He took it on and endured the CROSS because that was His goal all along: To be crushed under the weight of your sin so that YOU may LIVE. So, Friend...live.

Live while dying to yourself every day. Live while picking up your cross and following Him and say:

"YES, I will live out that purpose You have for me."
"YES, I will go through the process and allow you to heal me so you can use my story for your glory."
"YES, I will deal with my pain and forgive those who hurt me."
"YES, I will go where you send me."
"YES, I will lay down my life to glorify Christ."
"YES, I surrender!"

Friends, our goal is to DEAL, HEAL, and GROW in order to live a holy and set-apart life. You know what to do now! But if you need to remember, reread some chapters and do your cleaning work again.

It's part of running our race well. This commitment will position you to live a life that pleases Him and bring others closer to Him.

As part of your post-Soul-scan care, ensure you have a community that will hold you accountable for keeping things clean—keeping your *home* in alignment with God's word. Continuously fix your eyes on Jesus. Doing that will ensure you don't keep trinkets of anger, pain, and unforgiveness accumulating in the rooms of your soul.

You are free! Jesus has set you free! So, stay free, Sis!

You may be asking yourself: What now? What will the journey look like after I put this book down? What recommendations are there for me as I continue this inner healing and growth process? I got you!

Here are some fundamentals you will need to nurture from here on out.

Communication

Communicating feelings and needs can be very difficult for some people. It can take time to find out what is going on internally. Nevertheless, give yourself the space and permission to feel and communicate these feelings. If you find it difficult to pinpoint your feelings, check out the Feeling Wheel in the resource section. It is helpful to see several emotions laid out to identify the ones that resonate most for you at any given time. I would encourage you, my sweet friend, to share your thoughts and feelings with God, a trusted friend, or a licensed professional.

Self-care

If you haven't realized this by now, I don't know how else to tell you that the weight of unresolved pain can result in a devoted life to the idol of self-preservation, which leads to a *dead end*. We must realize that our lack of caring for our souls results in much more junk you'll have to sort through later. Self-care is a phrase and concept that has become very popular in our culture. I won't go into all the ways this concept has been twisted and distorted. What I want to highlight are how participating in activities that bring you life *is* caring for yourself. If you don't care for your mind, body and soul, who will?

Maybe you already try and do some type of self-care here and there. Maybe it's even sprinkled around your calendar but sometimes sometimes you miss two weeks. Then two weeks turn into three and so on and so forth. We feel the weight on our shoulders and forget how essential it is to take care of our basic necessities. For instance, when was the last time you drank water? And no I don't mean coffee I mean ACTUAL WATER! Are you showering? Getting out of bed doing something for you? Or are you drawing the blinds and letting the dishes pile on as you stay cooped up in your room? Friend, you must have a plan for real change to occur. Things like moving your body, having a good laugh or reading an exciting book are all things that have the potential to fuel your soul. Fan the flame that keeps you going. This is an essential part of your healing journey! Here are a few ideas of self-care that can help you cultivate a healthy and vibrant life:

- Drink water

- Take a bath

- Wash your hair/Get your hair done

- Dress up, just because

- Talk to a friend

- Go to counseling

- Get a massage

- Get a "mani-pedi"

- Read/listen to a book

- Go on a walk or run

- Ride a bike

- Spend time out in nature

- Explore a new city

- Go to a museum

- Listen to uplifting music

- Dance/Move your body

- Surround yourself with lifegiving people

- Watch a comedy movie, etc.

The point is to carve out a time to do something for you to care for yourself. If God commands us to love our neighbor as ourselves, let's be sure to follow that command all the way through. In order to love others best, we must learn to love ourselves. (Matthew 22:39 ESV)

Your Story is Needed

I know it might sound scary to you, but on the other side of your "yes," women are waiting for your story. And they need a safe place.

Your healing can be the key someone else needs to unlock faith and hope that God can do the same in their lives. 2 Corinthians 1:3-4 ESV says:

Blessed be the God and Father of our Lord Jesus Christ, the Father of mercies and God of all comfort, who comforts us in all our affliction, so that we may be able to comfort those who are in any affliction, with the comfort with which we ourselves are comforted by God.

How else would you know the comfort of the Almighty without needing it first. Because you've experienced and received comfort, you will have something to offer another hurting woman around you. You can share the good news. You are able to make His name great by sharing what He's done for you.

And they overcame and conquered him because of the blood of the Lamb and because of the word of their testimony, for they did not love their life and renounce their faith even when faced with death.
Revelation 12:11 AMP

One major proof of overcoming and growing beyond it is the fruit that's produced from your process. Your testimony is fruit that can feed others!

Remember several chapters ago when we talked through the story of the lame man Jesus healed near the pool of Bethesda? After this man received his healing, he went into town and told everyone about the great miracle Jesus had done in His life. Because of his proclamation and testimony, many people came to know Jesus.

Your story (testimony) is just as important!

Friend, there is a purpose for your healing. There is power and purpose in your story. You have not endured the heartaches in life this long for no reason. Before God formed you, He knew what you would go through and how this would grow you and impact those around you. With Christ's many healings and miracles, I'm sure people became intrigued, encouraged, and developed outrageous hunger to meet Jesus and experience His power! Sis, *you* are God's vehicle to draw others to Himself.

Sharing the breakthroughs you've had in your life, the healing you've experienced, and the freedom you now have in Christ is the greatest gift you can give others. Don't be a hoarder of your healing. **Give it away!** Spread the good news. Share the work of Christ in your life! We are quick to spread bad news reports, Hollywood (and all-too-personal) dramas, or the latest season's most-watched game score! How about we course correct and share the great works of our God? Make an impact by sharing the spiritual foods you've just gained.

Inside of you, you have access to a grand garden. This is now a greenhouse filled with healthy vegetation. Friend! Will you share?

I pray that you return to this book and remind yourself that Jesus is the only refuge for your soul. Only He can satisfy your thirst to belong, to be accepted, to be loved, to be cherished, to be seen and heard. In Him, you find wholeness. I'm proud of you for saying *yes*. I'm proud of you for going there. And if you didn't, that's okay too. When you *do* open yourself up to the healing found within the Healer, you will be immersed within the living waters of Himself when you come up from being immersed in ALL that He is and ALL He has to offer you. No matter how often you scan your soul, your perspective will change because there is ALWAYS something new for you to find. Now that you've started this journey, you will never be the same again because you will constantly experience transformation and renewal with each soul scan you do from here on out.

Mini Scans

Are you in the practice of keeping up with your routine pap smears, mammograms, physicals, etc.? Some women are diligent about it and make sure to schedule these because they realize how important it is to keep up with the state of their health. Some are just not that interested. I know of a woman who went years without getting any of her *goods* checked. We constantly encouraged her to get it together and take care of herself. She finally went and we were all stunned by the news she shared. The doctors had found cancer in her uterus. This quickly became a painful and scary process where big decisions needed to be made. What I learned was that things can change in an instant or they can change gradually. But if you are not in the habit of going for routine checkups, you may be shocked at the wave of medical needs you may come up against (seemingly all at once). This method may end up creating a huge load of turmoil in your soul that possibly could have been avoided.

Sister-friend, it doesn't have to be that way! Your soul is too valuable, and it's worth being tended to. Let this be a priority to you to routinely dedicate a time where you evaluate the state of your soul. Allow the Holy Spirit to be your doctor and show you areas that need His touch. Do not let ignorance get the best of you. Allow the knowledge, wisdom and application to bring the fruit of overall health.

He never gives up on you.

Christ has empowered us to break the hold of darkness, not just for ourselves, but for people we are divinely assigned to. If we are purposeful, we can break old narratives that keep us in bondage and create a new pattern and example for others to follow. Don't waste your life marinating on lies, worries, and fears. Stand in truth. Be empowered to take a stand and share the gospel of Jesus through how you live your life.

May your souls be set on fire! May your souls reflect the wonders of God. Love greatly, give generously, live boldly, and let your souls display what healing and freedom look like—for real.

You've done great work! Now keep it going, and watch how the Lord will continue to give you great victories to celebrate! Most importantly, don't keep this to yourself. Pay it forward! Share this book with other sisters who need a Soul Scan, and pray for their victories. Thanks for journeying with me Sis. Keep up the great work!

Chapter 11 Challenge: Post Soul Scan Plan

Create a plan for yourself. Write it down. If your plan includes reaching out to accountability, church community, counseling, etc. Collect it here and make the call. Set yourself up for success by writing the vision and making it plain (from Habakkuk 2:2).

_____

_____

_____

_____

_____

_____

_____

_____

_____

_____

_____

_____

_____

_____

_____

_____

_____

_____

_____

_____

Resources

Resources

TO HELP YOU IN YOUR SOUL SCAN JOURNEY

FEELING WHEEL

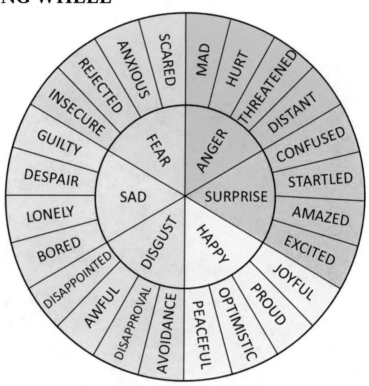

Using a tool like The Feelings Wheel can help you to get better in tune with yourself and your feelings. It can be a great tool for communication or even journaling.[1]

---

1. https://www.calm.com/blog/the-feelings-wheel

PRAYER MODELS
Five Prayer Models:

Here are five prayer models you can use to grow your relationship with God. ACTS, PARTS, Five-Finger, TRIP, Divine Reading (from bobyoungresources.com)

ACTS

A - Adoration: praising God for who He is
C - Confession: owning our sins
T - Thanksgiving: thanking God for all he has done
S - Supplication: prayers of request for ourselves and others

PARTS *of Prayer*

P - Praise
A - Ask
R - Repent
T - Thank
S - Share

FIVE-FINGER *Prayer*

- *Thumb*: pray for those closest to you

- *Pointing finger*: pray for those who guide us: teachers, doctors, counselors, and mentors

- *Middle finger* (tallest one): pray for those who lead us: government, civic, and business leaders, police, and firefighters

- *Ring finger* (weakest one): pray for those who are vulnerable: the poor, sick, disabled, infants, homeless, the powerless, the persecuted

- *Pinky* (the smallest, the least): Pray for me

Take a TRIP with God

T - For what am I Thankful?
R - What do I Regret?
I - Intercession—for whom do I need to pray?
P - What is my Purpose or Plan?

BIBLE STUDY METHODS:

"Here are a few methods from the Bibleway Gateway Blog.[2]

The Inductive Method

The Inductive Bible Study Method is a process by which you make observations of a passage and draw conclusions from those observations. The questions at the heart of this approach typically follow the five Ws (and one H) approach many of us learned in elementary school:

- *Who* (who is speaking; who is the intended audience; who is present in the moment, etc.)

- *What* (what is this passage about; what problem is this addressing; what is happening; what is being said; what commands need to be obeyed, etc.)

- *When* (when is this event taking place?)

- *Where* (where is this event taking place, where does it fit in the larger context of the book and Scripture?)

---

2. https://www.biblegateway.com/blog/2023/03/6-bible-study-method s-you-need-to-know-and-try/

- *Why* (why is this message needed, why is it relevant today?)

- *How* (how does this change what I know about God and humanity; how do I apply this to my life so that I can live more faithfully as a follower of Jesus?)

Many popular Bible study methods are variations of this tried-and-true approach (including many on this list). It's also important to note that an inductive Bible study doesn't require asking all of these types of questions every time.

All you need are the passages that help you to best understand the meaning of the message and apply it.

The Text Method

The TEXT Method is an accessible and memorable Bible study approach using four steps:

- **T**alk to God in prayer before you read.

- **E**ncounter God and humanity in Scripture as you reflect on two simple questions: What does this passage say about God, and what does it say about humanity?

- e**X**amine your heart, considering what needs to be confessed, added, taken away, or maintained as a follower of Jesus.

- **T**alk to God and others, thanking God for what he has shown you in Scripture, and sharing what he's shown you with someone else.

This method was introduced in The TEXT, a Bible designed for teens, young adults, and new believers, and can be practiced in a verse-by-verse or topical approach.[3]

The Verse-mapping Method

The verse-mapping method of Bible study allows you to study the historical context, transliteration, translation, connotation, and theological framework of a verse in the Bible. After choosing a verse (or verses) to study, do the following:

- Write out your chosen verse(s)

- Write them in at least two other translations (Remember, you can read a verse in multiple translations using Bible Gateway's free tools)

- Circle keywords to look up in the original languages and write down the definitions, synonyms, and root words

- Explore the meaning and message of the verse or verses as you consider the people, places, and context involved, and make connections to other relevant passages and concepts in Scripture (the cross references in your Bible are ideally suited for this)

- Write a 1–2 sentence summary of what you learned and consider how you can apply it

The Topical Bible Study Method

As the name suggests, this method helps you to explore in-depth a specific topic or concept within Scripture. To put this method into practice, follow the following steps:

- Choose a topic you want to explore, perhaps a theological concept or aspect of how we're meant to live as God's people

- Look up references to this topic (an exhaustive concordance is a helpful tool for this)

- Choose the verses you wish to study

- Ask questions about the topic

- Read the verses and see how they address your questions

- Summarize your conclusions

- Write out your application

The Character Study Method

Similar to a topical study, this method focuses on a specific biblical character to learn about how God worked in and through that individual and apply what we discover to our lives. Character studies involve the following steps:

- Choose the biblical character you want to study

- Find the relevant passages about him or her

- Read your passages, and consult additional Bible study tools like Bible dictionaries, to learn everything you can about this character (the trustworthy questions who, what, when, where, and how will serve you well here)

- Find the application points for your life

The S.O.A.P. Method[4]

#1 – S.O.A.P Inductive Bible Study Method

Nobody seems to know who came up with this method. But there is no doubt the most popular inductive Bible study method. SOAP has four basic steps:

- *S – Scripture* – Read the scripture portion you intend to study. Write down the specific passage that stands out to you. You can write out the part that stands out to you.

- *O – Observation* – Zoom in on the passage. Ask questions and answer them. What do you notice? Who wrote this? Why? Are there any repetitions?

- *A – Application* – Make it personal. How does the passage apply to your life right now? What changes do you need to make? What action does God want you to take?

- *P – Prayer* – Present your requests to God based on what has been revealed to you in your study. Confess where you have not been walking aright and ask God to help you apply His Words to your life in meaningful ways.

---

4. https://faithgateway.com/collections/love-god-greatly-bible

#2 – S.O.A.K. Inductive Bible Study Method

SOAK was developed by .[5] She created it as a tool that women can use to "soak in" God's word. Like SOAP, SOAK has four steps:

- *S – Scripture* – Read the passage you selected and focus on one or two verses. Write them out in a journal.

- *O – Observation* – Write out one or two things you observed or noticed in those verses. Take note of commands or promises from God.

- *A – Application* – Personalize the scripture. Ask "What's this saying to me? What action do I need to take?

- *K – Kneel in prayer* – Go to God in reverence. While you don't have to kneel, the important part is reverence regardless of where you are. Write out some of your prayers as well if you can.

#3 – 5P'S Inductive Bible Study Method

The 5P's method of Bible study was developed by Priscilla Shirer for her personal use. Here are the five steps:

- *Position yourself to hear from God.* Find a quiet place away from the hustle and bustle of life.

- *Pore over the passage and paraphrase the major points.* The aim is to spend quality time in it. Immerse yourself into the passage and really meditate on it. Then, paraphrase the main

---

5. https://womenlivingwell.org/

principles. You can paraphrase each verse if you are working through a chapter.

- *Pull out the spiritual principles.* Think about what God is trying to teach you through these verses? A command to follow, promise to hold to your heart, and attribute of God he is trying to reveal?

- *Pose the question.* This is where it gets personal. Are you following the command? Keeping the promise? Do I believe what God has revealed about himself?

- *Plan obedience and pin down a date.* Develop a concrete strategy on how you will put those words into practice. Write it down if you need to.

WHO I AM IN CHRIST

These Words of Truth are to serve as addresses and receipts for what God says about us.

I Am Accepted...

- John 1:12 I am God's child.

- John 15:15 As a disciple, I am a friend of Jesus Christ

- Romans 5:1 I have been justified.

- 1 Corinthians 6:17 I am united with the Lord, and I am one with Him in spirit.

- 1 Corinthians 6:19-20 I have been bought with a price and I belong to God.

- 1 Corinthians 12:27 I am a member of Christ's body.

- Ephesians 1:3-8 I have been chosen by God and adopted as His child.

- Colossians 1:13-14 I have been redeemed and forgiven of all my sins.

- Colossians 2:9-10 I am complete in Christ.

- Hebrews 4:14-16 I have direct access to the throne of grace through Jesus Christ.

I Am Secure...

- Romans 8:1-2 I am free from condemnation.

- Romans 8:28 I am assured that God works for my good in all circumstances.

- Romans 8:31-39 I am free from any condemnation brought against me and I cannot be separated from the love of God.

- 2 Corinthians 1:21-22 I have been established, anointed and sealed by God.

- Colossians 3:1-4 I am hidden with Christ in God.

- Philippians 1:6 I am confident that God will complete the good work He started in me.

- Philippians 3:20 I am a citizen of Heaven.

- 2 Timothy 1:7 I have not been given a spirit of fear but of power, love and a sound mind.

- 1 John 5:18 I am born of God and the evil one cannot touch me.

I Am Significant...

- John 15:5 I am a branch of Jesus Christ, the true vine, and a channel of His life.

- John 15:16 I have been chosen and appointed to bear fruit.

- 1 Corinthians 3:16 I am God's temple.

- 2 Corinthians 5:17-21 I am a minister of reconciliation for God.

- Ephesians 2:6 I am seated with Jesus Christ in the heavenly realm.

- Ephesians 2:10 I am God's workmanship.

- Ephesians 3:12 I may approach God with freedom and confidence.

- Philippians 4:13 I can do all things through Christ, who strengthens me.

"The more you reaffirm who you are in Christ, the more your behavior will begin to reflect your true identity!" (From *Victory Over Darkness*, by Dr. Neil Anderson)

Spiritual Warfare Prayers & Declarations

Now that you are this far into the process, I invite you to pray the following prayers. Take a stand in the authority Jesus Christ has given you and pray the following prayers and declarations from John Eckhardt's book *Prayers that Rout Demons*. As you break these curses in prayer, picture yourself fully clothed in the Armor of God, breaking walls and strongholds in your life that need to be demolished and driving out the messengers of Satan that have overstayed their welcome so that Christ has a clear space to refurnish your inner home according to His will.

Are you ready? Let's do this!

- I break all generational curses of pride, rebellion, lust, poverty, witchcraft, idolatry, death, destruction, failure, sickness, infirmity, fear, schizophrenia, and rejection in the name of Jesus.

- I command all generational and hereditary spirits operating in my life through curses to be bound and cast out in the name of Jesus.

- I command all spirits of lust, perversion, adultery, fornication, uncleanness, and immorality to come out of my sexual character in the name of Jesus.

- I command all spirits of hurt, rejection, fear, anger, wrath, sadness, depression, discouragement, grief, bitterness, and unforgiveness to come out of my emotions in the name of Jesus.

- I command all spirits of confusion, forgetfulness, mind control, mental illness, double-mindedness, fantasy, pain, pride, and memory recall to come out of my mind in the name of Jesus.

- I break all curses of schizophrenia and command all spirits of double-mindedness, rejection, rebellion, and root of bitterness to come out in the name of Jesus.

- I command all spirits of guilt, shame, and condemnation to come out of my conscience in the name of Jesus.

- I command all spirits of pride, stubbornness, disobedience, rebellion, self-will, selfishness, and arrogance to come out of my will in the name of Jesus.

- I command all spirits of addiction to come out of my appetite in the name of Jesus.

- I command all spirits of witchcraft, sorcery, divination, and the occult to come out in the name of Jesus.

- I command all spirits operating in my head, eyes, mouth, tongue, and throat to come out in the name of Jesus.

- I command all spirits operating in my chest and lungs to come out in the name of Jesus.

- I command all spirits operating in my back and spine to come out in the name of Jesus.

- I command all spirits operating in my stomach, navel, and abdomen to come out in the name of Jesus.

- I command all spirits operating in my heart, spleen, kidneys, liver, and pancreas to come out in the name of Jesus.

- I command all spirits operating in my sexual organs to come out in the name of Jesus.

- I command all spirits operating in my hands, arms, legs, and feet to come out in the name of Jesus.

- I command all demons operating in my skeletal system, including my bones, joints, knees, and elbows, to come out in the name of Jesus.

- I command all spirits operating in my glands and endocrine system to come out in the name of Jesus.

- I command all spirits operating in my blood and circulatory systems to come out in the name of Jesus.

- I command all spirits operating in my muscles and muscular system to come out in the name of Jesus.

- I command all religious spirits of doubt, unbelief, error, heresy, and tradition that came in through religion to come out in the name of Jesus.

- I command all spirits from my past that are hindering my present and future to come out in the name of Jesus.

- I command all ancestral spirits that entered through my ancestors to come out in the name of Jesus.

- I command all hidden spirits hiding in any part of my life to come out in the name of Jesus.

AMEN.

CONGRATULATIONS SIS... **YOU DID IT!**

You prioritized your relationship with the Lord and took time to *deal, heal, and grow.* I am so proud of you. I knew you could do it!

This is only the beginning. God has so much in store for you. The journey doesn't end here. I pray you continue to walk with the Lord into all He has for you. Keep this conversation with Jesus going, and don't allow the enemy to distract you. God is with you, and He's got you.

Your Sister in Christ,

Vanesa

Made in the USA
Columbia, SC
27 May 2025